309

MIRACLES

Geoffrey Ashe

MIRACLES

ROUTLEDGE & KEGAN PAUL

London and Henley

First published in 1978
by Routledge & Kegan Paul Ltd
39 Store Street,
London WC1E 7DD and
Broadway House,
Newtown Road,
Henley-on-Thames,
Oxon RG9 1EN
Set in Intertype Times Roman
and printed in Great Britain by
Lowe & Brydone Printers Limited
Thetford, Norfolk

ISBN 0 7100 0039 1

Contents

1

Magicians and Talking Animals

What is a miracle?

The simplest answer would be, 'Nothing at all. They don't happen.' But that answer sidesteps the question. There is not much point in denying them – or affirming them, either – without some sort of definition. You have to know what it is that doesn't happen, before you can even say it doesn't. Many people, after giving the matter a little thought, might come up with a negative notion rather than a positive one. Roughly it would be that miracles are 'impossible' events, which were once ignorantly supposed to happen, but which science has now disproved and banished, so that we no longer need to bother about them.

Strangely enough therefore, in view of that prevailing impression, it was a writer with a passion for science – the chief founding father of science-fiction – who proposed one of the few would-be definitions which a general reader is likely to come across. He put it in a short story called *The Man Who Could Work Miracles*, and, more surprisingly still, he later picked on this as his own favourite among the dozens he had written.

I refer of course to H. G. Wells. The story was published in 1897 and filmed during the thirties, an enduring classic of trick photography. Its hero, George McWhirter Fotheringay, is a perfectly ordinary person. One evening he is chatting with friends in a pub when the subject of miracles arises. An unbeliever himself, he defines a miracle as 'something contrariwise to the course of nature done by power of Will'. As an example, he points to a hanging oil lamp and tells it to turn upside down and go on burning with its flame pointing downwards. To the company's alarm, it does.

Gradually he grasps that in some unknown way he

has become omnipotent. While he is making cautious experiments, a policeman interferes. Mr Fotheringay tells him to 'go to Hades', and promptly finds himself alone. (Distressed at what he has done, he presently transfers the policeman to San Francisco.) A clergyman persuades him to use his gift for the benefit of mankind, and he begins improving the neighbourhood. He extends the railway, drains a swamp, improves the soil on a farm, and cures the Vicar's wart. These projects are carried out in the course of a night. Needing more time for undisturbed planning, Mr Fotheringay tries to postpone sunrise, commanding the earth to stop rotating. It does – whereupon all movable objects, himself included, are flung off by their own inertia and hurtle through space.

His final horrified act of power is to restore the universe to the exact state it was in at the beginning of the story, with one difference. This time he must not be able to work miracles. He can still order the lamp to turn over, but it won't. So life resumes its course as if nothing had happened, with the thaumaturgic upset, and all memory of it, blotted out.

It is a brilliant little fantasy. How about the definition, though – 'something contrariwise to the course of nature done by power of Will'? Is that what a miracle is supposed to be? If it is, then discussion is surely at an end. There is certainly no record of a super-magician like Mr Fotheringay in real life. But let us look at some of the world's miracle-stories, beginning with the oldest, and see whether they actually are like Wells's, and whether the people who told them were thinking of the same thing.

Homer, the earliest European author whose works survive, has an event in his epic *The Iliad* which we might feel inclined to count as a miracle. The Greek warrior Patroclus, a friend of the hero Achilles, has borrowed Achilles's chariot and horses, gone off to fight the Trojans, and been killed. Achilles prepares to ride out

8

in the chariot himself and avenge his friend's death. He tells the horses to take better care of him than they did of Patroclus. Whereupon something most unusual happens. One of them, Xanthus, begins to speak in a human voice. Here is Homer's account of what follows, slightly compressed.

> Xanthus had lowered his head, so that his mane came tumbling from the yoke-pad by the yoke and swept the ground. He said: 'Indeed, my dreaded master, we will once more bring you safely home today. Yet the hour of your death is drawing near; and it is not we who will be the cause of it, but a great god and the strong hand of Destiny. You too are doomed to fall in battle.'
>
> Achilles was angry with him and replied: 'Xanthus, you waste your breath by prophesying my destruction. I know well enough that I am doomed to perish here, far from my dear father and mother. Nevertheless, I am not going to stop till I have given the Trojans their bellyful of war.'
>
> With that, he raised the battle-cry and drove his powerful horses to the front.

Two things stand out in this strange incident. First, there is not the slightest suggestion that Achilles himself has anything to do with it. He does not 'will' the horse to speak, and he could not if he tried. We are told, in fact, just before the lines quoted, that Xanthus was enabled to retort to his master by the goddess Hera. The other point of interest is that although it takes a goddess to make such a thing happen, Achilles does not show surprise. He simply gets angry and answers back. The weird warning makes no difference, and Hera's miracle, if that is what we should call it, falls flat.

But should we call it a miracle? Isn't it just a fairy-tale marvel, coming down from a folklore world where unseen beings and talking animals were all in the day's work? At any rate there is no superhuman act of will, nor is there the sense of anything being 'contrariwise to the course of nature'. In pursuit of the genuinely miraculous, and the proper meaning to give to that word, we must press on further.

Can we trace any line of development from early tales

of the Xanthus–Achilles type? There is another story we can compare Homer's with, and one that is close enough to make comparison interesting. The Bible too has a talking animal. In *Numbers* 22 King Balak of Moab, alarmed at the Israelites' advance into his country, sends a deputation to a man named Balaam asking for help. Balaam is a magician or soothsayer, and the king wants him to put a curse on the Israelites. After some persuasion, and ominous dreams, Balaam agrees to accompany the envoys. He rides back with them on his donkey. God, however, opposes Balaam and sends an angel to stand in the path with a drawn sword. The donkey sees the angel, Balaam does not. At the first and second apparitions, the donkey gets troublesome and Balaam hits her. The third time, when the angel stands in a narrow defile where there is no room to turn aside, she lies down and refuses to budge.

> Balaam's anger was kindled, and he struck the ass with his staff. Then the Lord opened the mouth of the ass, and she said to Balaam, 'What have I done to you, that you have struck me these three times?' And Balaam said to the ass, 'Because you have made sport of me. I wish I had a sword in my hand, for then I would kill you.'

Thus far we seem to be in the same folklore atmosphere as before. The donkey speaks by divine inspiration, the Lord's instead of Hera's. Balaam, like Achilles, is annoyed rather than surprised. But this time the story is not finished. After a second exchange between beast and rider, the marvel goes further.

> The Lord opened the eyes of Balaam, and he saw the angel of the Lord standing in the way, with his drawn sword in his hand; and he bowed his head, and fell on his face.

Why, says the angel echoing the donkey's words, has Balaam been hitting her? She has done him no harm. On the contrary, by refusing to go forward she has saved his life. The angel would have killed him.

Then Balaam said to the angel of the Lord, 'I have sinned, for

I did not know that thou didst stand in the road against me. Now therefore, if it is evil in thy sight, I will go back again.' And the angel of the Lord said to Balaam, 'Go with the men; but only the word which I bid you, that shall you speak.'

The angel has to appear in person, God's recognised spokesman, to rub it in. But the shock, if slightly delayed, does occur. Balaam realises that something bizarre and awful is going on, and he is shaken. The author has moved out of the naïve folklore world into another, a world of more sophisticated reactions and weightier meanings. Even his fairy-tale effects now have symbolic value. The donkey, which seemed so refractory, was actually doing her rider a good turn. So likewise, the Israelites do not deserve Balaam's enmity. When it comes to the point, the Lord prompts him again, and to the king's fury he blesses them instead of cursing.

Given this altered milieu, the strange occurrence has a genuinely miraculous air. In itself it is much the same as Homer's. But Balaam is different from Achilles, because – if not instantly – he recognises the portent as such, and knows that he must take its extraordinariness to heart, as a sign from heaven. He is smitten with wonder. And that is what the word 'miracle' implies. It is Latin-derived and based on the adjective *mirus*, 'wonderful'. A miracle is, by definition, something you wonder at.

That of course is far from being the whole story. To begin with, the converse is not necessarily true. There are plenty of things which inspire wonder but are not miracles. The word's derivation has caused it to be spread too widely, both in everyday use and in the language of poetry and emotion. We say 'If he's ready in time it will be a miracle,' meaning only that it will be astonishing. Drugs such as penicillin were at first nicknamed 'miracle drugs' because their effects were so startling by contrast with any known before. Again, it is quite common to find people speaking of 'miracles of nature' or 'miracles of life', with no further implication

11

than that the stars are beautiful or the structure of living bodies is complex. Such phenomena cause wonder, and rightly, but it is not that sort of wonder. Walt Whitman's poem *Miracles* voices the wonder while regrettably confusing the terminology.

> Why, who makes much of a miracle?
> As to me I know of nothing else but miracles,
> Whether I walk the streets of Manhattan,
> Or dart my sight over the roofs of houses toward the sky,
> Or wade with naked feet along the beach just in the edge of the water,
> Or stand under trees in the woods,
> Or talk by day with any one I love, or sleep in the bed at night with any one I love,
> Or sit at table at dinner with the rest,
> Or look at strangers opposite me riding in the car,
> Or watch honey-bees busy around the hive of a summer forenoon,
> Or animals feeding in the fields,
> Or birds, or the wonderfulness of insects in the air,
> Or the wonderfulness of the sundown, or of stars shining so quiet and bright,
> Or the exquisite delicate thin curve of the new moon in spring;
> These with the rest, one and all, are to me miracles,
> The whole referring, yet each distinct in its place.
> To me every hour of the light and dark is a miracle,
> Every cubic inch of space is a miracle,
> Every square yard of the surface of the earth is spread with the same,
> Every foot of the interior swarms with the same.
> To me the sea is a continual miracle,
> The fishes that swim – the rocks – the motion of the waves – the ships with men in them,
> What stranger miracles are there?

Whitman's attitude to the world is valid and splendid, but if everything is a miracle, nothing is. In Franz Werfel's novel of Lourdes, *The Song of Bernadette*, an educated romantic says to the local peasants, 'Are there not miracles all around us? Is not the moon in the sky a miracle?' One of them replies, 'The moon, monsieur? But we see her every night.' The peasants know better than the visitor.

When Wells's Mr Fotheringay speaks of miracles as 'contrariwise to the course of nature', he is – to that extent – on the right lines. A miracle is not thought of as just wonderfully good or exciting. Even to say that it is wondered at for being unusual is far too mild. It must fly in the face of pooled human experience. It must be an exception to the laws which seem to govern the world. There will be more to add before a full definition can take shape, but the first key word to seize hold of is *exception*.

It follows that a frequent error must be cleared out of the way. The idea of miracles is not backward or pre-historic, but fairly advanced. There has to be a rule of law before there can be exceptions to it. A human society must have firm notions of nature's regularity – through watching seasons and the heavens, through techniques such as stock-breeding and agriculture – to reach a point where an exception, real or imagined, is going to be a theme for awestruck amazement.

In the lands of the Middle East and Mediterranean, where western civilisation has its roots, that point was reached only after a long phase of transition from barbarism. The atmosphere of earlier times is hard to recapture. Order was recognised in the way the world functioned, but it was thought of in terms of magical and psychical forces rather than law, and the whole human environment was so full of strangeness that nothing could be radically surprising. Hence, there could not then have been any meaning in the word 'miracle'. The passing of that transitional era, the change-over to a state of affairs in which exceptions *would* be surprising, seems to have been linked somehow with a change in society's sexual bias. Whether or not women ruled in the older world, as some feminists claim, they had a major share in the all-important arts of magic. They thus inspired more reverence than in later times, and divinity itself was predominantly female rather than male. The source and presiding power of life was then a Great Goddess under many guises and names

– Ishtar, Astarte, Cybele, and so forth. She was the All-Mother and the bestower of inspiration and immortality. While she reigned, humanity and divinity were felt to be close, intermingling. But during the second millennium BC, male deities such as Zeus rose to ascendancy. The female was cut down, subordinated, split up into smaller goddesses.

In her older world, with its magical and psychical order and its interpenetration of realms, almost anything could happen. It was through the rise of her supplanters the male gods that the notion of cosmic law, and the regularity of material nature, very gradually took hold. Under the rule of the male, with his more legalistic mind, nature slowly came to be seen as constant in its workings. The exceptional event was at last made to stand out as a miracle.

Some investigators believe that the change was more than a change of outlook. They accept that in the earlier, anything-can-happen phase, the phase of female magic and mystery, events which we would now think of as extraordinary would not have been so thought of; but they suspect that this is not all. According to their theory, such events did actually happen more often, and were far less out of line. Part of the reason why they were not thought of as extraordinary was that in many cases, they were not. ESP, telepathy, and kindred phenomena which we might now label as paranormal or supernatural, were familiar facts of life. When the male gods took command imposing their new law and order, the world was not only seen as more predictable and mechanical, it actually became so. Human beings atrophied somewhat in their psychic faculties. Things which had been a matter of course for their ancestors were now abnormalities to be wondered at.

A shift undoubtedly did take place towards a smaller and sadder concept of human destiny. Faith in immortality waned. In the era of the female, death had not been the end. In the era of the male, generally speaking, it was. The future state dwindled into the feeble and

14

bloodless shade-existence which was all that most Greeks and Middle Easterners could look forward to when they died. That bitter loss helped to sustain a nostalgia for the lost age of the Goddess, which, many centuries later, was to play a part in one of the most spectacular chapters in the whole history of the miraculous.

For the moment, however, we are still many centuries BC. Whether or not human beings altered, the mental atmosphere certainly did. But it did not alter overnight. In Homer, while Zeus has already become the chief deity and the surviving female powers are subject to him, there is (as we have just seen) plenty of the old anything-can-happen spirit lingering on. The gods are capricious rather than orderly, and may affect the world and its mortal inhabitants in all sorts of ways. Homer describes even quite natural events in these terms. Thus, when a man decides to take some action, Homer is apt to say that a deity, such as Zeus or Athene, 'put it into his mind' to do so-and-so. Behind the deities is Fate, but that is inscrutable and still has nothing to do with laws of nature. So the horse's breaking into speech fails to startle or influence Achilles; it is merely a trick such as gods are prone to; and the event falls short of being a true 'wonder'.

The author of the Balaam tale is a trifle further advanced in this respect. He believes in the God of Israel, a Lord who has no use for the ancient mysteries, who dictates rigid laws such as the Ten Commandments, and who exerts his power in a much more single-minded style than the gods of Greece. If a donkey talks, therefore, it is an extraordinary event, and the Lord must have arranged it specially for a purpose. It comes with a jolt, and has to be taken seriously. The Lord, unlike Homer's gods, is an all-male sovereign without female distractions, and not capricious.

Though the book of *Numbers* is still pre-scientific, it helps in getting rid of the delusion that scientific thinking supersedes miracles. We would be nearer the truth if

15

we were to say that scientific thinking made them possible in the first place – as an idea, that is, whether valid
or mistaken. To conceive miracles at all, a society has to
be at least on the road to science: to a conviction that
there are normal ways in which things happen, together
with a mental scheme of what normally does happen,
which will make any exception conspicuous and startling. So long as gods were the prime causes of the way
the world functioned, the God of Israel could take his
worshippers further towards that view of it than
Homer's wayward Olympians could. Greek science,
when it came, outstripped any science achieved by ancient Israel, but it was the work of Greeks who had left
the Homeric myths behind, and moved towards a higher
notion of order which they often related, as the Israelites did, to one supreme God.

Today, we must discuss miracles in the same spirit if
we are to discuss them usefully, and ask whether they
occur. We must think of them as exceptions, events that
refuse to fit the pattern of 'what normally happens'.
Science in its modern developments has made that pattern more exact than it ever was under the gods, or even
under the One God of Israelite faith. It has not changed
the basic position about exceptions. Nor, as we shall see,
has it proved them to be impossible.

A miracle means an exception, but not any exception as
such, anything defying our knowledge and mental
habits.

Imagine that you are looking at a billiard table, level
and undisturbed. On the centre spot is a red ball. Suddenly it begins moving by itself and rolls into a pocket.
If a ball were actually to behave like that, it would be an
exceptional event and very hard to account for, but not,
in itself, a miracle.

Scientific credibility is not the main issue. Nineteenth-
century physics would have declared that such a thing
could not happen. Since then, 'laws' of a rigid and im-
mutable kind have been replaced by statements of prob-

16

ability. It is wildly unlikely that a ball would start rolling by itself, and, apparently, aim itself. Yet some freak molecular lurch, perhaps in the air on one side of it, might – in theory – give it an impulse towards the pocket. That, however, is a quibble. The thing may be possible, but it is so far-fetched as to be right outside experience, and outside the assumptions of scientific method. While asserting the reign of probability rather than fixed law, and allowing the improbable, scientists recognise an *excessive* improbability which, if encountered, compels re-thinking or a suspicion that there is something wrong. A teacher using the billiard table for a demonstration in mechanics would take it for granted that the ball would, in practice, keep still. If it did not, he would conclude at once that something had interfered, without even considering freak molecular lurches. As far as being exceptional goes, an uninterfered-with, self-starting, self-aiming ball would qualify. It would be special pleading for a physicist to argue, 'Well, anything *can* happen, so there aren't any exceptions, so this isn't a miracle.'

The real question, however, is about the observer rather than the fact. If the ball did roll into a pocket unaided, and that was all, would you feel the kind of wonder that is supposed to attend the miraculous? You would be surprised, but would you be surprised in that way? You might be scared, but would you be thrilled or awestruck? Hardly. The event would be meaningless. It would convey no message, apply to no situation, reveal no unseen hand. A miracle is not merely an exception, but an exception with a point. It has a bearing on human life, and this is so because there is some sort of agency behind it which human beings can relate to themselves. It is an *ordained* exception, ordained for a reason.

By whom or what? By a Wellsian 'power of Will'? Would the billiard ball's antics become miraculous if Mr Fotheringay were under the table willing it along? Early miracle-stories never suggest anything of the kind. Homer's scene of Achilles and his horse, though pre-miraculous in itself, foreshadows them all in that respect. The marvel is not worked by Achilles but by a divine being. That goes on being true, with variants, when the Greeks after Homer do achieve a notion of miracles. The gods, who are the causes of whatever order the universe has, are also the causes of such events as seem to depart from it. They have a monopoly of interference and adjustment.

We possess, for instance, the fascinating record of a sort of Greek Lourdes, the temple of Asclepius at Epidaurus in southern Greece. Asclepius was the god of healing. Originally a deified hero, he never attained equal rank with the Olympians, one of whom, Apollo, was said to be his father. But his cult grew to a point where he was a fully accredited deity with shrines of his own. The one at Epidaurus flourished from the fifth century BC onward. It was much more than a building. Walled round like a cathedral precinct, it had spacious grounds with open-air altars and groves of trees, and it included not only the temple itself but baths, a theatre, and sheltered colonnades where pilgrims could sleep. To a large extent the place was simply a hospital, with priests of the god as doctors. But when a sick pilgrim stayed for a while within the precinct, the god might visit him and help.

The Epidaurian Temple Record is a list of cures, and of miracles going further than cures, which took place there. While the shrine functioned, accounts of these were inscribed on tablets along the inner wall of a colonnade, so that pilgrims could read them and be encouraged. A patient would make a donation to the shrine (not necessarily in cash; he could, for instance, paint a picture) and sleep in one of the places allotted. Asclepius might then appear to him in a dream.

Sometimes the dream-imagery was straightforward. A man named Euhippus, who had a spear-point lodged in his jaw, dreamed that the god took it out and went away with it, and in the morning it was gone. But sometimes the visitation was more symbolic. A man infested with lice dreamed that Asclepius went over him with a broom. And sometimes the process was more complicated. Pandarus of Thessaly, disfigured by a mark on his forehead, bandaged his head as instructed by the god, and presently found the mark transferred to the bandage. Then a friend who was similarly disfigured borrowed the bandage; but he had cheated the shrine of a promised offering, and when he removed the bandage he found it was clean again, and he had Pandarus's mark on his forehead beside his own. The pilgrimage could also be made on someone else's behalf. The mother of Arata of Laconia, who suffered from dropsy, slept at the shrine herself and dreamed that Asclepius cut off her daughter's head and drained away the liquid. Arata, at home, had the same dream and was well again when her mother returned.

Most of the recorded cures are no more than cures, which might be put down to natural causes, or to skilful treatment by the priests. Others, such as the disappearance of the spear-point and the transfer of Pandarus's mark, at least seem miraculous, and the latter has a moral as well. The record shows that the miracles were few, and even the simple cures were not numerous. There were enough to sustain hope and faith, and to attract funds for maintenance. But obviously, if the priests had been able to improve Asclepius's score themselves, or even pretend to have done so in the past, the number claimed would have been greater. It was clearly understood – too clearly to leave room for major deception – that beyond a certain point, human agency had no power in the matter. If Asclepius chose to work a miracle, then he would, but it was the god's doing and he did not often choose.

The dramatist Euripides lived and wrote when Asclepius's temple was in its prime. His attitude to the gods was sceptical. Yet in his handling of Greek myth the treatment of miracles is exactly the same. The most supernatural of his plays is *The Bacchae*. In this there is a long speech by a royal messenger, telling the King of

Thebes about the Bacchanal women revelling on the mountain in Dionysian ecstasy. It is as full of marvels as any passage in Greek drama. The women, according to the messenger, draw miraculous food and drink from the earth, and cannot be harmed. But Euripides never hints for one moment that they are witches performing magic in their own right; in the age of the Male, that view of the matter is no longer to be contemplated; the god Dionysus does it all for them, communicating his power through the sacred thyrsus or wand which his worshippers carry.

> One would raise
> Her hand and smite the rock, and straight a jet
> Of quick bright water came. Another set
> Her thyrsus in the bosomed earth, and there
> Was red wine that the God sent up to her,
> A darkling fountain. And if any lips
> Sought whiter draughts, with dipping finger-tips
> They pressed the sod, and gushing from the ground
> Came springs of milk. And reed wands ivy-crowned
> Ran with sweet honey, drop by drop. . . .
>
> The village folk in wrath took spear and sword
> And turned upon the Bacchae. Then, dread Lord,
> The wonder was. For spear nor barbèd brand
> Could scathe nor touch the damsels; but the Wand,
> The soft and wreathèd wand their white hands sped,
> Blasted those men and quelled them, and they fled
> Dizzily. Sure some God was in these things!

Those are the words of a poetic dramatist re-creating a legend. But the historian Herodotus, writing of real events within living memory, has at least one spectacular marvel which he thinks of in very much the same fashion. When the Persians invaded Greece, he relates, a force marched on Delphi to plunder Apollo's shrine. The Delphians consulted the oracle and Apollo replied that he could protect his own. As the Persians approached, sacred armour from inside the temple came out by itself; rocks broke off Mount Parnassus and started an avalanche, burying many of the Persians; and two gigantic warriors appeared and attacked them. The survivors fled in panic, pursued by the ordinary soldiers of Delphi. Herodotus warns his readers that this is what he was told, not what he saw. But he did see the rocks lying where they had rolled down. Apollo had protected his own.

Even in a later, decadent era, when Greeks were far more superstitious and credulous, they seldom lost sight of the fundamental point. A time came, for instance, in the last twilight of paganism before the Christian triumph, when many statues of the gods were solemnly credited with coming to life and performing quasi-human actions. But it was never imagined that a statue in itself had supernatural properties. Once again, the god was the cause. Whatever power the statue showed came (it was agreed) from the invisible divine being it stood for, who, for reasons of his own, made it perform.

Outside Greece we have an older and greater story than any of these, probably the oldest anywhere with a strong miraculous content. It draws vital distinctions which the Greeks, with all their love of clarity, were never precise about, and in fact tended to blur as they declined towards superstition themselves. This is the Hebrew narrative which includes Balaam's dialogue with the ass as one of its episodes: the saga of the Israelites' departure from Egypt, and their conquest of Canaan, the Promised Land.

The Biblical book of *Exodus*, which opens the story, is the part of it with the most significant miracles. At the outset the Israelites are in Egypt, enslaved. One of them, Moses, escapes to Midian in Sinai and marries into a local family. When he is tending sheep on the lower slope of Mount Horeb, the Lord speaks to him from a burning bush, and tells him to go back to Egypt and lead his compatriots out of bondage. Moses is bewildered at being chosen like this, and pleads that he is unequal to the task. What proofs can he offer of such an unheard-of mission, either to the Israelites themselves or to their master Pharaoh?

The Lord said to him, 'What is that in your hand?' He said, 'A rod.' And he said, 'Cast it to the ground.' So he cast it to the ground, and it became a serpent; and Moses fled from it. But the Lord said to Moses, 'Put out your hand, and take it by the tail' – so he put out his hand and caught it, and it became a rod in his hand – 'that they may believe that the Lord, the God of their fathers, the God of Abraham, the God of Isaac, and the God of Jacob, has appeared to you.'

Again, the Lord said to him, 'Put your hand into your bosom.' And he put his hand into his bosom; and when he took it out, behold, his hand was leprous, as white as snow. Then God said, 'Put your hand back into your bosom.' So he put his hand back into his bosom; and when he took it out, behold, it was restored like the rest of his flesh.

'If they will not believe you,' God said, 'or heed the first sign, they may believe the latter sign. If they will not believe even these two signs or heed your voice, you shall take some water from the Nile and pour it upon the dry ground; and the water which you shall take from the Nile will become blood upon the dry ground.'

Still Moses demurs. He protests that he is not good at making speeches. The Lord tells him to rely on his brother Aaron, who is, and will be ready to help. So Moses returns to Egypt. Aaron acts as his spokesman, the 'signs' are duly performed, and the Israelites believe. Pharaoh, however, who is not present at the demonstration, is unimpressed by the brothers' message. He grants them an audience but says he knows nothing of their God, and accuses them of encouraging the Hebrew slaves to be idle and discontented. The only result of the interview is that the slaves' tasks are increased. Moses complains to the Lord, who replies that he must go to Pharaoh again, and promises – without explanation – that release will come.

Now the word 'miracle' occurs.

The Lord said to Moses and Aaron, 'When Pharaoh says to you, "Prove yourselves by working a miracle," then you shall say to Aaron, "Take your rod and cast it down before Pharaoh, that it may become a serpent." ' So Moses and Aaron went to Pharaoh and did as the Lord commanded; Aaron cast down his rod before Pharaoh and his servants, and it became a serpent.

Pharaoh's rejoinder should be carefully noted.

> Then Pharaoh summoned the wise men and the sorcerers; and they also, the magicians of Egypt, did the same by their secret arts. For every man cast down his rod, and they became serpents. But Aaron's rod swallowed up their rods.

Nevertheless Pharaoh does not yield. Moses, still acting in blind obedience to the Lord, takes his rod and strikes the water of the Nile, which turns to blood. 'But the magicians of Egypt did the same by their secret arts.' Next, a similar gesture brings a plague of frogs. Again the magicians match him. But when the dust turns into a swarm of gnats, they try but fail. From that point onwards, Moses and Aaron inflict worse and worse disasters on Egypt without further competition. When they bring an epidemic of boils, we are told that the magicians suffered like all the other Egyptians. Pharaoh tries concessions and compromises, without success. After a further series of blows, culminating in the death of the first-born son in every family, he at last surrenders and the Israelites leave. Soon he regrets it and pursues them with a chariot-borne army, only to succumb to the crowning miracle of all: the Red Sea divides and the Israelites walk across on the sea-bed, but when the Egyptians follow, the water flows back and they are drowned.

Clearly there has been a contest in wonder-working which Moses has won. But what exactly has he been doing? When the opening gambit with the rod is called a miracle, does that mean only a stronger kind of magic? No. The difference is crucial, and it is not an afterthought of theologians in later ages; it is brought out again and again, even here in what reads like a fairly primitive tale. Pharaoh's wise men and sorcerers do tricks 'by their secret arts' – the phrase is used every time. Moses, by contrast, is anything but a wise man. He has no idea how the phenomena happen. The Lord issues orders and he obeys. Until the battle begins and gives him confidence, he is frightened and unwilling.

The miracles that happen for Moses are prodigies decreed by the God who controls nature, to overawe the oppressors of his chosen people. Thus far the Hebrew and Greek conceptions are on much the same lines. Miracles come from a divine source. But Pharaoh's resistance, with its attempts at counter-action to discredit the miracles, introduces a further issue. It is not the resistance of a rival divine system. We might expect to hear of the gods of Egypt opposing the Lord, as pro-Trojan gods fight pro-Greek gods in Homer's epic, but we never do. The mighty Egyptian pantheon – Ra, Osiris and the rest – never takes the field at all. Egypt's gods are mentioned in only one sentence, when the Lord promises to execute judgment on them (12:12). The authors of the story regard them as powerless idols. Pharaoh's champions against Moses are not priests but wizards. When they admit defeat after the plague of gnats, they confess the difference between their marvels and his: 'This,' they tell Pharaoh, 'is the finger of God.'

Miracles are not magic. The Egyptians' tricks are merely routine effects which they know how to produce to order 'by their secret arts', only surprising to anybody else because the arts are kept secret. They are the same in kind as the tricks of a modern theatrical illusionist. And that would be true even if these magicians were real magicians, performing feats by methods unknown to science. It makes no difference how we conceive them to be doing their tricks, they are not working miracles. The Jewish historian Josephus, re-telling the story in the first century of the Christian era, makes Moses say to Pharaoh: 'Indeed, O king, I too disdain not the cunning of the Egyptians, but I assert that the deeds wrought by me so far surpass their magic and their art as things divine are remote from what is human. And I will show that it is from no witchcraft or deception of true judgment, but from God's providence and power that my miracles proceed.'

Miracles are not magic; or to put it more accurately, they are distinct from magic as magicians (truly or

24

falsely) claim it to be. Magic is supposedly a set of techniques for causing strange events, or achieving abnormal knowledge. Human beings, it is alleged, can learn and apply these techniques, consciously, deliberately, and knowing more or less what will happen. Hence magic belongs to the same regular order as science. Indeed the higher magic overlaps science: alchemy passes into chemistry, astrology into astronomy. The magician professes to do what the uninitiated cannot, and are amazed at. But he does it himself. Even if he enlists the aid of spirits or demons they are under his command. There is no question of making exceptions in the system. On the contrary, the magician's universe is governed by law in all its workings, though some of the laws may sound absurd or fanciful; and the techniques for controlling the system can be taught.

The orthodox magician, however lofty his pretensions, is on the same side of the fence in this respect as the conjuror. They may look very much alike. In 1856 French rule in Algeria was threatened by marabouts – Moslem holy men – who gained influence over the people by displays of wonder-working, and stirred up revolt. The French Government sent out the conjuror Robert Houdin, who did better tricks and destroyed the marabouts' influence. To an Algerian, it might have been hard to tell whether Houdin was exposing the marabouts as mere conjurors, or working real and superior magic himself.

Kindred doubts have arisen with a modern illusionist, Uri Geller, who (unlike Houdin) insists that his feats *are* more than conjuring. The Geller debate opens up such topics as ESP, psychokinesis, parapsychology. As with magic, so with these. If they are real, and if they are what believers claim them to be, they are not miraculous either. What is alleged is that they reveal unknown human powers, which belong to the natural order and can perhaps be brought within the domain of science. That is the position, for example, of Arthur Koestler in *The Roots of Coincidence*. Lyall Watson, the author of

25

Supernature, maintains throughout that the puzzling facts he is presenting are not supernatural. Parapsychologists from J.B. Rhine onward have tried to study ESP by experimental methods. By doing so they are saying in effect that they do not think ESP phenomena are miraculous. The main point of an experiment is that it should be repeatable and, broadly speaking, predictable, governed by rules and not outside them.

Notice that I am careful to insist on the 'if'. These things are not miraculous . . . if they are what believers claim them to be. Neither are feats of magic . . . if they are what magicians allege. It remains a question whether the magicians and parapsychologists know, or have ever known, what they are talking about. Some of their phenomena may be genuine, yet their explanations may still be mistaken. We shall come back to this. But a miracle is certainly otherwise. It is not thought of as caused by human beings applying 'secret arts'. It is not even thought of as due to some unfathomed power which a few human beings can exert at will without comprehension. That is where the Wellsian definition goes wrong, so that Wells's story, though a superb piece of fun, is irrelevant. The agency that causes a miracle is something OTHER, transcendent. It has a relationship to the human world and its needs, but is not of that world, and affects it from outside. It is 'higher' and cannot be compelled, or predicted, or fully understood, though it may perhaps be invited. It creates special cases, and by doing so it communicates, helps or harms.

The best short definition of a miracle is *a divinely ordained exception* – provided that in using the word 'divine' we are not question-begging. It is true that miracles have been traditionally ascribed to gods, and, above all, to the One God of Jewish and Christian faith. But to speak of a miracle as a divinely ordained exception should not be made to imply that such divine beings exist as imagined. Nor, conversely, should miracles be

26

made to depend on their existence. You may say, 'Well, obviously it's no use talking about miracles unless you can first prove that God exists to work them.' Or you may say, 'Well, I don't believe in God, so it's no use talking to me about miracles.' Neither comment should be allowed to close the discussion. The word 'divine', as used here, refers simply to the Something Other. People have interpreted this as God, or as a realm of gods, so 'divine' seems the best term. They may have been wrong. Their gods may be only symbols. What the idea of the miraculous does imply is that at the very least they are symbols of Something Other which is actually there, even if we have no name for it. You may believe in this or you may not, but the only way of cutting off miracles at the source (so to speak) would be to *dis*prove it. I do not see how that could be done, and so long as the question remains open – no more than open – miracles can go on being discussed.

P. D. Ouspensky, a follower of the esoteric teacher Gurdjieff, recorded some of his meetings with the Master in a book called *In Search of the Miraculous*. At the beginning of this book he tries to explain his use of the word. Everyday life, he argues, is 'a thin film of false reality'. Beyond it there exists 'another reality from which, for some reason, something separates us'. The miraculous occurs when we are in contact with this unknown reality, so that for a moment its workings are made visible to us. Ouspensky conveys the same notion without bringing in gods, or God. Still his other and truer reality could fairly be called divine.

One thing more, which is important for understanding, though scarcely part of a definition. Behind miracles is the belief that the Something Other does exist, does weave irregularities into the pattern; and this belief has a rebellious, defiant flavour. Whatever the Something is, it raises man above his apparent fate.

The progress of social organisation, the growth of the scientific conception of an ordered universe, have never been unmixed blessings. Subjects of the ancient empires

27

felt hemmed in by relentless destiny, oppressed by remote powers, dragooned and thwarted and hurt by 'the way things are'. For most of them, organised society meant servitude and taxation and war. For most of them, nature's laws meant sickness and old age and death, with little left of the older faith in immortality. In consequence a belief in Something Other, able to snap the chain, helped many to rise above defeat and despair. Hence some of the major miracles of religion. By all the rules, the Israelites in Egypt were enslaved for ever, but Moses came to save them with a God who could destroy Pharaoh's certainties. Gods of healing such as Asclepius kept hope alive when doctors could do no good. Greater still would be a triumph over the arch-certainty death; therefore Christ's supreme miracle, surpassing all others, was to be the Resurrection.

In all these cases and many more, the stories do involve personal deities. Especially in Judaism and Christianity, miracles are often presented as 'signs'. Their purpose is, precisely, to fortify believers with an assurance that God is there, and all-powerful, and protective or loving, able to rescue them from encompassing misery and doom. Bernard Shaw in *Saint Joan* takes this point acutely and then pushes on beyond it (or makes a character do so) to a conclusion which orthodoxy could hardly accept: that a miracle need not be a real one at all, so long as the assurance of a saving divine reality comes through. The Archbishop of Rheims is speaking:

A miracle, my friend, is an event which creates faith. That is the purpose and nature of miracles. They may seem very wonderful to the people who witness them, and very simple to those who perform them. That does not matter: if they confirm or create faith they are true miracles.

To which a courtier objects:

Even when they are frauds, do you mean?

The Archbishop replies:

28

Frauds deceive. An event which creates faith does not deceive: therefore it is not a fraud, but a miracle.

Again, a few speeches farther on:

> Miracles are not frauds because they are often – I do not say always – very simple and innocent contrivances by which the priest fortifies the faith of his flock. When this girl picks out the Dauphin among his courtiers, it will not be a miracle for me, because I shall know how it is done, and my faith will not be increased. But as for the others, if they feel the thrill of the supernatural, and forget their sinful clay in a sudden sense of the glory of God, it will be a miracle and a blessed one.

In other words, even a conjuring trick can actually *be* a miracle, if it is done, so to speak, in a miraculous atmosphere. We can hardly go along with such a confusion of terms, but Shaw brings out an important aspect of the subject. And he helps us, perhaps, to understand the psychology and to see how the miraculous (or at any rate the quasi-miraculous) can be thought of without a full-fledged personal deity.

Because it can be. Given a milieu where religion carries little weight, the same impulse is apt to show itself in the allure of gambling. For millions of people, the psychological equivalent of a miracle is a big pools win – the utterly exceptional yet not inconceivable event, which holds out hope of escape from the day-to-day grind, the routine of assembly line or office. If all gamblers relied purely on chance, the parallel with the miracles of religion would go no further than that. But in fact the supernatural part, the Something Other, is often still present. It appears in the countless superstitions which gamblers cherish, the fancies about an occult factor that can bias the laws of probability, and make exceptions in their favour. Lady Luck is seldom a goddess literally believed in (though she once was, under the name Fortuna), but what she stands for is plainly outside the rational scheme of things.

I have before me a newspaper advertisement by an astrologer and dealer in 'charms'. At the top is a picture of a couple opening a gate which leads out of a gloomy street into a sunlit park. Under this is the caption

PUSH OPEN *YOUR* LUCKY GATE!

Next comes a testimonial from somebody who has actually had a pools win. 'Mrs A.T. of Worcester gave *her* lucky gate a push when I told her she was due for a change of luck.' The claims to inside knowledge that follow are based chiefly on astrology and numerology ('Lucky Numbers'), and to that extent they are pseudo-scientific. With a full reading, however, says the astrologer, 'I also give a golden Egyptian Scarab Seal Charm, worshipped for over 5,000 years in the mysterious East as KING OF ALL THE CHARMS!' Why should any readers desire or wear such an object? The only motive that makes even nominal sense is a lingering notion of supernatural powers, which will exempt them from the normal workings of chance, and pay dividends . . . literally.

2

The Chosen

As a matter of history, miracles are bound up with religion. But they do not figure equally in every religion. In some, they are few and marginal. In others, while alleged marvels are abundant, it is doubtful whether they should be called miracles. The theme has its own logic, and can only be satisfactorily approached by one path: that of the single great tradition in which the idea of the miraculous is fully worked out. This is the one we have already paused upon, which begins in the Old Testament with the religion of ancient Israel, and then passes into Judaism and Christianity.

The reason why the Judaeo-Christian scheme takes the notion furthest lies in the way it conceives the Something Other. Its God is unlike the gods of Greece.

Though Greek gods were credited with acts which might be called miracles, the nature of those acts was never very precise, and advancing Greek thought tended to leave them behind rather than attempt to define them. The gods' relationship to the world of mankind was, in the last resort, ambiguous. They were indeed 'other', but not entirely so. Of course they were superior, superhuman, immortal. They were set apart by having a place of their own, Olympus. This was not the literal mountain so named, but a domain above in a sort of stratosphere, the *aither*. Yet however inaccessible their dwelling might be, it was never conceived as truly supernatural, truly outside. It was still within our universe, and so were the gods, who did not even wield unrestricted power, but were checked by Fate. Was an event genuinely miraculous if it was due merely to one part of the cosmic system, a deity, tinkering with another part such as a sick pilgrim in a temple? The Greeks never sorted that question out. To them it was not interesting enough. When their paganism expired, Asclepius's cures and Apollo's repulse of the Persian army slipped quietly into limbo.

For the Israelites, divinity was a different matter. There was only one higher power that counted, Yahweh to give him his Hebrew name, the Lord God of Moses. What Moses himself really said about his God, we cannot be sure. But the Old Testament books in their present form were composed centuries afterwards, in the light of the way his message had been developed by later teachers, especially the prophets such as Isaiah. It is clear that in any period which can fairly be called historical, Israel's God was different from the rest with a total difference. His 'otherness' was radical. He had existed before the world, and was his own master, not limited by any Fate or hemmed in by any divine colleagues. He had made the world alone and he now ruled it. But he transcended it, standing completely outside as the gods of Gentile nations did not. Hence, any marvels he might cause in his world were true and meaningful exceptions, not generated within the system but ordained from beyond; and he alone could ordain them. The Israelites were his chosen people. The Old Testament describes many marvels worked by the Lord on their behalf, such as those attending their flight from Egypt.

Israel's thinkers, and the Jewish rabbis who later expounded their ideas, never went all the way to the concept of a world running like a machine, with its Creator quite distinct from it. In a scientific age we may feel obliged to picture the universe as ruled by natural laws, with miracles (if any) coming in as divine intervention ... not to say interference. In the Old Testament milieu this is not yet possible. It is realised that nature does, on the whole, behave regularly and reliably, but that is because God governs it thus, and not by whim. Apart from human beings – who are free to rebel and often do – all things, animate and inanimate, obey him. In general they have their orders. But he can, at will, override those orders by special decree, and that is how he works miracles. According to one Jewish tradition, he foresaw at creation what miracles would be required in the course of history, and prearranged them with the natural objects concerned. At his request they all promised to behave exceptionally at the proper juncture. The sea, for instance, agreed to draw back when the Israelites escaping from Egypt should want a safe passage. Once they were across, it would revert, so to speak, to business as usual.

In the light of science, Jewish and Christian theologians today can no longer take such a naïve view. They have to accept the natural order as a reality (albeit a God-made reality) which science discloses, and then draw a line marking off God and his special acts as supernatural, beyond the reach of science entirely. They differ as to how and where they should draw it. We need not get involved in their arguments. The sole question that matters here, as we approach the mass of biblical miracle-stories, is whether this accommodation can stand up at all and allow such stories to be true.

To some extent in the eighteenth century, and to a much greater extent in the nineteenth, a notion took hold that science – or, at least, the style of thinking which underlies science – had progressed to a point where it disproved the biblical miracles; where, in fact, it exploded miracles altogether. The philosopher David Hume argued that a report of a miracle could never be credible, even with living witnesses, much less with witnesses dead thousands of years. The reason he gave was that the presumption that 'nature must always behave regularly' is now known to be stronger than any possible testimony to its behaving otherwise. Hence, twenty witnesses might swear that they had seen a corpse come to life. But since all experience assures us that corpses don't do this, the rational course is still to reject the miracle, and explain away the witnesses' story as best we can (they were all mistaken; they were all lying; or whatever other escape route we prefer, however far-

33

fetched, because *anything* is more believable than a break in the normal sequence of nature). In due course came the biblical critics such as Ernest Renan, who, in 1863, produced a best-selling *Life of Jesus* spun entirely out of the axiom that miracles don't happen, so that the Gospel narrative must be re-written to get rid of them.

A careful reader might have had his doubts, even then. The authors who made the most stir were apt to be inconsistent themselves, or to sidestep the real issue. Hume, for instance, upset his own case by proving in another book that the 'presumption' of nature always behaving regularly has no logical basis. Renan betrayed the fact that he did not even know what a miracle meant, by refusing to admit the possibility unless somebody worked one to order under controlled conditions – a test that might be applied to a magician, but hardly to God.

Today, the idea that 'miracles don't happen' and that 'science disproves them' is still current. However, it is pure dogma, and must be cleared out of the way to assess the miracles of scripture. The theologian's position may or may not be right, but it can be sustained. Science is about what normally happens. It is grounded on generalisations from the study of many cases. A miracle is an exception, a maverick event. It is outside the net of generalisation. Therefore, it is outside the net of science.

Dogmatic unbelievers are still known to use the argument that miracles cannot happen because the laws of nature cannot be broken. If a single event were to depart from the rules, they say, the effects would pile up and the whole universe would slide into chaos. Such an argument belongs more to the Victorian era of strict determinism than to our more bewildering age of nuclear physics. But even in the Victorian era it was dubious.

In the first place, an exception does mean an exception. If something were to be right outside the normal rules, science would have no means of predicting its consequences. The universe might slide into chaos, but then again it might not. In the second place, since God – in the Judaeo-Christian scheme – is himself the source of the laws that govern creation, he can suspend their working. The classic talking point here is the prodigious miracle in *Joshua* 10:12–14, when Joshua needs more time to defeat the Amorites, and the sun halts in the sky by God's command, giving an extra spell of daylight. Objectors (some perhaps remembering Mr Fotheringay) urge that the sun could only have stopped if the earth stopped turning, and if it did, every loose object would have been thrown off. But why? If God can suspend natural law in one respect, he can suspend it in others. He could make an exception as sweeping as he chose, not only stopping the earth turning, but cancelling the inertia of the movables on its surface.

Which is not to defend Joshua's miracle as a fact of history, but merely to point out that there is no snap logical refutation, even of such a wild wonder as this. Science – and more broadly, a scientific mode of thinking – can be applied to scripture in all sorts of ways. It can certainly show that the Old Testament is not a literal record of fact from beginning to end. Astronomy and geology refute the creation story. Archaeology and ethnology refute some of the history. Fundamentalism will not work. Fundamentalism, however, is based on a misapprehension in any case, and a fairly recent one. Early Jewish and Christian writings on the Old Testament, while they do lean towards naïve belief, show a sufficient awareness that it is not all meant to be taken literally. Science, therefore, cannot simply smash it to pieces on general principles. Any given passage, including the miracle-stories, must be carefully weighed and evaluated before any judgment can be passed. Again there are no snap answers.

Though science cannot disprove miracles as such, it can disprove particular ones, and that is a fact to bear in mind when examining scripture. The way in which it does so raises the question of a converse – whether it could ever prove a particular miracle. Obviously it

35

could not do so directly, for the reason already seen, that miracles are outside science. Yet its critical methods have a bearing in a positive as well as a negative sense. Today, if a miracle is alleged, science can probe the evidence. It may dispose of the miracle by showing that the evidence is too flimsy, or that it has serious gaps. If the evidence is good, science may still show that the event can be explained by natural causes. This is the procedure laid down for the Medical Bureau at Lourdes, and it dismisses nearly all Lourdes cures as non-miraculous. Rarely, however, very rarely indeed, the facts are well attested and no natural explanation emerges. Then permission is sometimes given for a miracle to be claimed.

Whether or not the Lourdes procedure is followed strictly enough (we shall be coming back to it), the method is valid, and correct for the Bible too so far as it can be used at such a distance of time. We should always remain alert to every possibility. As a rule, we should resist miracles to the last. Yet we should be prepared to accept that they may sometimes be proved – or, at any rate, very powerfully recommended – by the lack of any alternative. Rational inquiry may show (*a*) that something is a fact and (*b*) that no known natural explanation will cover it.

So how should we assess the miracles in the Old Testament? Did any of them actually happen, or is their value confined to helping us to think about the miraculous? The first thing to grasp is that the stories are of different types. They can be classed roughly under six headings.

If we start from the least substantial, the first type is the plain *fairy-tale*. A story falling under this head is, to all appearances, simply folklore. The Old Testament has very little such matter, because of its earnestness, its constant concern with the relationships of God and mankind. Even the most primitive legends, when used, are nearly always given meanings and morals. Perhaps the nearest thing to a pure fairy-tale incident is the death of the hero Samson, ancient Israel's strong man. He has a final access of super-strength which enables him to pull down the Philistines' temple, crushing himself with his enemies in the ruins (*Judges* 16:28–30). As an earlier passage makes clear, his strength is correlated with the length of his hair. He loses it when Delilah has him cropped, and his demolition feat becomes possible when, unnoticed by the Philistines, the hair grows again. Even here the Lord is explicitly involved. Samson prays before assailing the temple pillars, and seems to be made stronger than the actual length of his hair would warrant. But a divine miracle based on the hair motif surely need not be taken very seriously. Another episode with a fairy-tale quality is Jonah's adventure inside the 'great fish' (*Jonah* 1:17–2:10), though attempts have been made to detect a deeper significance in it.

Second comes the *tale with a purpose*. A story in this class carries more weight then the preceding kind, but still has a fictitious or mythical air. It is best taken not as literal history but as myth or fable or allegory, told to teach some lesson or make some point. We may view its inclusion in scripture as a proper use of imagination, or as priestly mendacity, according to taste. The affair of Balaam's ass, though employing a fairy-tale motif, fits better here than under the first heading. Such an occurrence would be a miracle if it happened, and, as we saw, it is presented as such with that understanding. However, it need not be regarded as more than a fable showing Yahweh's power to master a heathen magician. Much the same applies to other miracle-stories in which the God of Israel confounds the Gentiles. He throws the impious builders of Babel into linguistic disarray (*Genesis* 11:1–9). He shatters a Philistine idol when the captured Ark of his Covenant is placed in its shrine (*I Samuel* 5:1–5). He keeps Shadrach, Meshach and Abednego unharmed in the furnace where Nebuchadnezzar has had them cast (*Daniel* 3:19–30). The Babel story, a myth explaining the existence of many languages, is used here to display Yahweh's superiority. The other stories have the same object, as their conclusions prove – the Philistines and Nebuchadnezzar are overawed. Again there is no real need to look for more. We are dealing with saga material and literary material, rather than history.

The case is likely to be similar with the prophet Elijah's celestial ascent is a fiery chariot (*II Kings* 2:11–12). Josephus, the historian, says simply that he vanished. His exit by chariot looks like a tale told to account for his disappearance, in such a way as to underline his value in the sight of the Lord, who presumably caught him up to heaven.

A third type of Old Testament miracle-story might be described as *history improved*. This is the most important. The story is based on something real, or probably real. We have a hard core of history. But the event has been mythified, growing in the telling, and becoming more marvellous. Most of the public miracles which the Lord works for Moses belong in this class. Thus, several of the plagues he inflicts on Egypt may quite well have happened; perhaps over a longer period, perhaps in a less overwhelming way, but with enough cumulative force to convince the Egyptians that their Hebrew slaves were bringing them bad luck. Even some of the odder plagues, such as the turning of water into blood, are possible (in a sense) without any literal miracle. Nile water can be reddened by a micro-organism, or by soil deposits carried down from Ethiopian lakes.

As for the Israelites' passing through the sea on foot, when Moses leads them out of Egypt (*Exodus* 14:21–9), this reflects a known possibility. While the Red Sea could not have parted for them without a real and major miracle, its presence is probably a geographical error. They crossed the 'sea of reeds' or Papyrus Lake. This has been altered by the Suez Canal, but before the digging of the Canal it was very shallow. At certain times of low water the fugitives could have walked across. A sudden change of wind and level could then have bogged any Egyptian chariots that might pursue. Such a rescue would have been ample for the faith of Israel to grow around. There is concrete evidence for it. Moses's sister Miriam raises a song of triumph afterwards (*Exodus* 15:21) – 'Sing to the Lord, for he has triumphed gloriously; the horse and his rider he has thrown into the sea' – and the archaic language suggests that this song is the oldest thing in the Bible, and could well have been made up on the spot. The Egyptians had no cavalry then, but 'rider' may mean 'chariot-rider'.

What we have at the heart of such a tale is a real event which was amazing and seemingly providential, but could still have happened without a miracle. If it did, the more fantastic touches – the sea's parting and rising like a wall on each side, the drowning of the pursuers by its return – are meant to magnify the event and emphasise the Lord's hand in it. (I have heard an orthodox Jew aptly call them 'de Mille effects'.) Similarly the fall of the walls of Jericho, which collapse at the sound of Israelite trumpets after a week of ritual marching round (*Joshua* 6:1–21), may be based on a tradition of an earthquake. Much later in the Old Testament (*II Kings* 19:32–5) we find the Lord saving Jerusalem from Sennacherib's army, in response to the prayers of King Hezekiah, by sending an angel to kill 185,000 of the Assyrian soldiers. Sennacherib's siege is attested by independent record. The army may have been crippled by an epidemic; the angel with his immense massacre is surely a 'de Mille effect', an image of the wonders which the Lord works for his people. In this instance as in others, there *may* have been a full-fledged and tremendous miracle. It cannot be disproved. But Assyrian sources confirm only that the siege was given up. A smaller, non-miraculous happening, afterwards heightened to glorify the God who rescued Jerusalem, is all that is required to account for the facts.

Fourth comes the miracle-story which can be viewed as *truth, but demystifiable*. With a number of incidents which are made to sound miraculous, it is in the telling rather than the actual events. They may have happened very much as described, but without any miracle. The authors wish to present them as special manifestations of divine power. People present at the time – some, at any rate – would have understood their nature. We can guess at this ourselves by discounting the presentation, and simply trying to interpret the data.

The Lord speaks to Moses from a bush which burns without being consumed (*Exodus* 3:2–4). It could have been a gas-bush or dittany accidentally ignited. When the Israelites are wandering thirsty in the wilderness, Moses strikes a rock and water flows from it (*Exodus* 17:2–6). He may have fractured a piece of limestone cliff-face, so as to give an outlet for an underground spring. Even in the notorious case of the sun stopping for Joshua (*Joshua* 10:12–14), the nub of the story is that he wanted, and got, a longer spell of daylight to conquer the fleeing Amorites. It may be that the pursuit drew his army out of a shady valley, where the sun was dropping behind the hills, into open country where it was still high. There is still some exaggeration, because we are told that the sun 'stayed in the midst of heaven' for 'about a whole day'. As to the main event, however, we may suspect that it is real but that its miraculous aspect is literary rather than literal.

Under the same heading we might, at discretion, list a few cases where tradition may have handed down an event as a miracle because someone used special knowledge or a special technique, which was unfamiliar at the time. To the expert it was not miraculous. To the onlookers it was. At least twice in Elijah's career, the prophet figures in an extraordinary scene which common knowledge today makes less extraordinary. When a boy dies, or is thought to have died, Elijah prays and 'stretches himself upon the child three times', whereupon the Lord brings him back to life (*I Kings* 17:17–24). Artificial respiration? Again, when Elijah confronts the prophets of Baal on Mount Carmel (*I Kings* 18:17–40), he demonstrates that Yahweh and not

40

Baal is the true God by an apparent miracle: in response to his prayer, the fuel under his sacrificial offering catches alight by itself. It is within credence that he used a burning-glass. Carmel, as a matter of fact, was one of the first places where glass was made. Of course there is no need to insist on such 'rational' explanations. The point is that with some of the Old Testament miracles, they do exist. We can, if we wish, believe the story yet reject the miracle, as being no more in reality than the author's omission of the explanation.

It is fair to distinguish a fifth class, which is like the fourth but not exactly the same – the story of an event which was *a genuine marvel at the time*. Arguably it not only happened as described, but, in that setting of date and place, was so far beyond anyone's comprehension that there was no way of accounting for it but super-human agency. The reason, however, was merely ignorance. Advances in knowledge would now enable us to explain it.

The Old Testament has few stories like this. Here and there, however, we come across an incident which has had to wait for the advent of science to be de-supernaturalised, but which now can be. The Lord sends an evil spirit to torment King Saul, taking possession of him and causing inexplicable conduct (*I Samuel* 16:14, 18:10–11). Afterwards Saul has a terrifying meeting with a dead man, the former king-maker Samuel (*I Samuel* 28:8–20). In both cases, Israelite thinking can only handle the event as a divine visitation on an unworthy ruler. In both cases, being better informed about abnormal psychology, we are free to treat it as historical but due to mental unbalance. Plausibility is strengthened by the same man's being concerned in both. Psychological causes can account also for some of the bizarre experiences of the prophets.

And sixthly and lastly, after all these eliminations, must come the solid *miracle* where there is no other way of accounting for the data. Have we got anything left? Does the Old Testament offer a single story which meets the requirement? Almost certainly not. Its miracles are so distant in time, the testimony is so scrappy and uncritical, that we can justify classing all cases under the other five headings. In fact, several of the examples proposed here under the third, fourth and fifth may well belong further back, in the realm of imagination.

To say so is not to rule the miracles out finally. Possibly some are authentic after all. Possibly some did happen, and the non-miraculous version, though available, is wrong. Jews or Christians who wish to believe in them are at liberty to do so. Their belief, however, must be a matter of faith. They must not pretend that impartial logic supports them. The conclusion seems to be that while the Old Testament is very helpful indeed in thinking about miracles, or about reports of them, it supplies no convincing ones itself.

Yet this negative verdict is not the final word. It may be true that we can explain away every Old Testament miracle in detail. But they are components of a greater whole, and not the only components. This is far more than any of them, and more than the sum of all taken together. The historic phenomenon of Israel, viewed in its entirety, is much harder to account for by natural causes. To look no further, experts in comparative religion have signally failed to show how this tiny, mediocre, culturally poor nation produced a concept of deity, a series of prophets and a great literature, utterly unparalleled in other nations of the same kind (or bigger ones, for that matter). To the charge that the self-styled Chosen People were merely a swarm of semi-barbaric tribesmen, no different from the Moabites or Edomites, the Bible itself is a complete answer. We have no Bibles composed by Moabites or Edomites.

Israel created a religion which rose to unequalled heights of exaltation and influence, and, so far as we can make out, did not 'just grow' from the conditions of Israelite existence. It was, in fact, profoundly against the grain. In defiance of natural factors and desires, attested by continual lapsing into Baal-worship and so forth, Israel was repeatedly dragged back to that religion. There may be no case for any single miracle, for any single event in the Old Testament as an exception to the norms of the universe. Yet Israel-as-a-whole was an exception among the nations, a most mysterious one. That is proved by history, by anthropology, by any system of knowledge which can be applied as a test. Israel itself, well aware of its difference, claimed that this was ordained by its God, he who transcended nature – he who was the source, precisely, of the miraculous. Thus Israel's career might be interpreted as a sustained miracle in itself, going on for centuries.

Is the six-heading breakdown a mistake, which lets some vital factor slip through? Is the simple believer more or less right after all? To make sense of Israel's history, must we promote some of the marvels towards the literally-miraculous end of the scale, making that history more tangibly unique?

A well-instructed Jew, unless he belonged to the most strictly orthodox school of thought, would answer 'No'. To make Israel's uniqueness depend on miracles in detail would be to get the perspective wrong, and miss the main issue. The Lord may or may not have acted specially in special cases. In the life of his Chosen People he was acting specially all along, though not necessarily in the same style. Perhaps, when the Israelites were escaping from Egypt, the water did recede in a natural way. The point would not be that it receded, but that it receded at the moment when they wanted to cross. Or if you prefer, they were brought there at a moment when it was about to recede. In either case the synchronisation was the Lord's doing. Perhaps again, when Elijah's offering on Mount Carmel caught fire, he did use a burning-glass. But the Lord taught him how, or, at any rate, saw to it that he should know how.

The Old Testament itself never sharply isolates the miraculous. In fact, it never draws the modern line between 'natural' and 'supernatural'. God transcends his

43

creation and stands above it, but it does not run without him like a machine. Scripture gives us a panorama of God-acting-in-his-world both through habitual procedures which we call natural, and through special events of various kinds. Some of the latter, those we would call miracles, are plainly foreign to nature's system as he habitually arranges it. Others may not be exceptional in the same obvious way. Yet together they compose a vast pattern of contrivance. In traditional Jewish thought, it does not much matter which are which.

This remains a sound principle. Where religious belief can still make serious claims in accounting for the Israelite mystery, it is not by way of single overt miracles. Little is gained by debating whether an idol did or did not fall down when the Ark of the Lord was put in front of it. The case, rather, is for divine providence over a broader field. A major part of that will take the form of divine inspiration, as with the prophets. Overt miracles (if any) will lie within this larger scheme and must remain largely a matter of opinion, or faith.

A question better worth pondering is how we are to picture divine providence, or divine inspiration, without them. Can God be imagined as acting specially in his world in any way short of the outright miraculous? Is there an intermediate kind of event which is neither purely natural nor a total exception? That problem is not merely antiquarian, or confined to the study of the Old Testament. It raises, for instance, the whole issue of prayer. In 1940 many people in England prayed for the safe return of the army from Dunkirk, and regarded the calm weather for the evacuation as an answer. Yet nothing was observed which did not conform to meteorology. So did God step in or not? and if he did, how? And if he acted likewise for ancient Israel, could any number of non-miraculous 'special providences' add up to the apparent miracle of Israel itself?

Theologians have argued that God can intervene in the world and in human minds without actual miracle, because he is outside time as we know it. He foresees the situation, including any prayers which are offered up, and disposes natural causes from all eternity so as to bring about the result. A crude analogy would be the setting of an alarm clock. X knows that Y will need to be woken up early, so he gives him the clock, setting it to go off at six a.m. The clock ticks quietly through the night and then, at six, something happens meeting Y's need: the bell rings. This can be fully explained by the mechanism. All the same, it is X's doing. It would not have happened, and Y perhaps would have overslept and missed an appointment, if X had not foreseen the need and pre-arranged the mechanism accordingly. God can act thus, it is urged, and when he does there is no exception in nature. When he works a miracle, there is. On the alarm clock analogy, the miracle corresponds to X coming in at six and striking the bell himself with a hammer, by-passing the mechanism altogether.

This may or may not be a viable distinction. We shall be looking at it again. But the Old Testament does not draw it, any more than it clearly divides the natural from the supernatural. Though it includes so many events which, if real, were miraculous, it never separates the miracles from special divine action of other kinds. It lays unfaltering stress on God as their only source. God is Other. He is present in what we know as nature all the time, and its normal behaviour is due to him. Because he also transcends it as its maker and master, he can override his own rules. But whether, say, the inspiration of the prophet Isaiah did or did not require him to override them; whether he could or could not have pre-arranged the cosmos so that Isaiah would be inspired without miracle – these questions are over-subtle. Through his people Israel, and for them, the Lord works his wonders and they are wonderful indeed. That is the Old Testament's message on this topic. We must not press its authors for more exactitude as to which wonders are miracles and which are not. The finer distinctions, valid or otherwise, emerge later – chiefly among the Christians who come afterwards.

However, some of the authors do have a further idea, developing the theme in another direction. God may work several wonders – even a whole series – through a single member of the chosen community, moulding that community by making the person a living demonstration of divine power. The one so favoured never becomes a magician or super-being. He may, like Moses in the early chapters of *Exodus*, be reluctant and bewildered. At the utmost he prays, as Joshua does by implication when the Lord 'hearkens to the voice of a man' and stops the sun. But, through divine election, he is a person with whom wonderful events are associated. They happen in his presence. They attest what he is, and empower him to carry out some divine purpose.

Besides Moses, Elijah is a major instance. So is his successor Elisha, who carries on his witness against apostasy among the northern tribes, and is so constantly attended by marvels that he is closer than any other biblical figure to the wizards of folklore. It is not always easy to decide what to make of Elisha's feats. Some are slightly comic. One at least is more than slightly repellent. He performs several cures, and restores a dead boy to life. But he also (for example) makes a spring give drinkable water by throwing salt in it. He adds meal to a stew and thereby counteracts a poisonous herb. When a wood-cutter drops an iron axe-head in the river, he drops a stick at the same place and the axe-head rises to the surface. In each of these cases Elisha's use of a material adjunct strengthens the quasi-magical effect. Yet repeated allusions to his 'praying to the Lord' prevent a reader from long forgetting where the power comes from. This is true of his most notorious exploit, whatever it may be held to imply.

> He went up from there to Bethel; and while he was going up on the way, some small boys came out of the city and jeered at him, saying, 'Go up, you baldhead! Go up, you baldhead!' And he turned around, and when he saw them, he cursed them in the name of the Lord. And two she-bears came out of the woods and tore forty-two of the boys.
>
> (*II Kings* 2:23–4.)

Through Moses, Elijah and Elisha, and to a less extent through one or two others, Israel's tradition supplies a third factor in the miraculous, which persists later when miracles are better defined. So far we have had (1) the ordained exception, and (2) the transcendent Something – biblically speaking, God – that ordains it. These are the only essentials. But in the Old Testament, and increasingly thereafter, we also find (3), *the person in a special relationship with God:* so close to him, so much in harmony with him, that the miracles which God works through that person almost seem to be his own doing. He does not perform them by will-power or technique, and probably has no idea how they happen. Nevertheless they do happen, and set him apart.

Judaism – that is, the religion of the Israelites' Jewish heirs, developed from the Old Testament – made this idea more explicit, and carried it much further in its presentation of two leading figures. One was scriptural. The other was prophesied on scriptural grounds.

The first was Elijah. It will be recalled that in *II Kings* 2:11–12 he vanishes without dying, wafted out of the world in a literal or symbolic chariot. That is not the end of him, because in one of the last-written prophetic books (*Malachi* 4:5) God promises to send him to earth again. Jewish belief enlarged on scripture by making him the subject of an arch-miracle, which gave him a status above the rest of humanity. God had made him immortal, and allotted him a place of honour in heaven, where he still befriended the remnant of the Chosen People and interceded for them. He made secret return trips, to visit good Jews and bring them aid and comfort. He had appeared, it was whispered, in many forms – as a black man in one visit, as a woman in another. Legends of these adventures gave him three principal earthly roles: as a helper of the poor and humble, as a companion of scholars and sages, and as a rescuer from danger.

Subsidiary miracles sprouted from the main one of his continued life. God, it seemed, had given him virtual

47

carte blanche to perform them. One story told how Elijah had reconciled two learned men, Judah and Hiyya, who were not on speaking terms. He went to Judah disguised as Hiyya and cured him of toothache. From that moment they were friends again. According to another story, Elijah had averted disaster when a rabbi named Nahum incurred the wrath of the Roman Emperor. Nahum was appointed to bring the Emperor a casket of jewels as a gift from the Jews of his city. On the way, robbers stole the jewels and filled the casket with earth. When the Emperor opened it he thought the Jews had insulted him, and threatened a massacre. Elijah appeared disguised as one of his advisers, and told him that the earth was of a special kind known only to Jews. He should issue it to his troops, who were fighting to suppress a rebellion. They tossed it at the rebels, and it turned into showers of swords which routed them. The delighted Emperor gave the casket back to Nahum, filling it with jewels himself.

Elijah's most important task lay in the future. He was to return as foretold in *Malachi* and prepare the way for the Messiah, the other sovereign wonder-worker of Jewish lore. The Messiah was foreseen as an even greater God-favoured man. His title means 'Anointed'. Anointing is mentioned first in scripture as a ritual of kingship. From Saul onward, the monarchs of Israel were consecrated with oil and thereby enrolled as earthly deputies of the Lord. Later the word came to be used metaphorically, of divine choice for the carrying out of a special purpose. Later again, when the Jews were succumbing to Roman power, 'the Anointed' became a specific leader expected to arise to help them. At first he was pictured in fairly sober terms, as simply a descendant of David who would free Israel from alien dominance, in keeping with the Lord's pledges through the prophets. But as the alien dominance was imposed more and more firmly, the hope expanded and grew more flamboyant.

The Messiah, it was declared, would be 'girded with

stength' to 'shatter unrighteous rulers' in general and set up an everlasting kingdom, with all the Gentiles subservient to the Lord, and receiving the law from Zion. Astounding marvels would accompany his advent. Elijah would reappear as his herald, and assist him in his reign. The Messiah would give a great banquet for his followers ushering in an age of plenty. There would be a prodigious increase in the earth's fruitfulness, a blossoming of waste places, even a brightening of the sun. His enemies would be overthrown by fire and earthquake. With the more daring dreamers, he became the human protagonist in a total world-renewal. His reign would witness a resurrection of the righteous dead. God would transport their bodies to Palestine, and there Elijah would restore them to life, to enjoy a paradise called Gan Eden which would be planted in the east.

Not all Jews cherished such extreme visions, and those who did cherish them disagreed over the programme. But the yearning for the 'Anointed', the saviour, whatever the precise extent of his marvellousness, grew ever more potent. The promise of his glories lightened the burden of subjection to Rome, and remained a consolation after the hope of instant triumph had faded.

3

'God With Us'

Christianity began with a Jewish sect claiming that the Messiah – in Greek, the Christ – had actually come as prophesied, though not as expected. It was preached by the disciples of Jesus of Nazareth. He had been put to death under the Roman governor Pilate about AD 30. In spite of this they firmly declared him to have been the promised one. All their preaching, and indeed all the doctrine that followed on from it, was an attempt to spell out the meaning of an overwhelming experience they had undergone. Jesus, for them, had been like no other man. Even his crucifixion had confirmed his unique glory instead of exploding it, because he had not stayed dead. He had returned to life, and they had seen him and talked with him several times before his final disappearance from earth.

The first Christians were well aware that his career had not fitted the Messianic pattern. There was no resurgent Jewish kingdom. They gave Messiahship a new meaning. Christian teaching came to centre on the idea that God had fulfilled the prophecies, not simply by sending or 'anointing' a man, but by becoming one himself. This was the doctrine of the Incarnation. God was re-expounded as a more complex being, not one Person but a Trinity of three, Father, Son and Holy Spirit. The second Person, the Son, had been born on earth as Jesus the Christ. Jesus had been fully human, but also divine. The Gospel of Matthew applied prophetic texts to him, including one which said: 'His name shall be called Emmanuel, which means, God with us.' Instead of bringing political revolution, Christ was said to have brought a spiritual kind which was greater and more profound. Few Jews could acquiesce in such a surrender of their hopes, or in the concept of Christ's divinity which it was bound up with. Christianity was taken over within a lifetime by Gentile converts.

The Church's account of its own origins, as agreed upon during the later part of the first century AD, appears in the four canonical Gospels. (Others were composed, but rejected as spurious.) Here it is told how Jesus was born through a miracle, the Virgin Birth, and how he worked miracles at will during his public career. That, at least, is the implication everywhere except perhaps in one verse of *Mark* (6:5), which says that when he re-visited his home town, he 'could do no mighty work there, except that he laid his hands upon a few sick people and healed them' – the reason for his semi-failure being the unbelief of the locals. Even this, however, may refer only to an unsuitable atmosphere, to a moral im-possibility rather than a literal one. In all other texts he seems able to do anything, instantly, without any of the techniques associated with magic. For Christians who told such stories of him, there was no break with the prin-ciple that God alone worked miracles, because Jesus *was* God – the Son of the heavenly Father – as well as man.

The divine act which set his career in motion, his conception in the womb of the Virgin Mary, marked his uniqueness. On the one hand he was human, physically and solidly human, being born of woman. On the other hand he was also more than human, because the normal process of procreation had been replaced by a divine fiat. The embryo had appeared in Mary's womb by the will of the Heavenly Father without impregnation of any kind. Jesus was the son of no man.

At the other end of his earthly career was the Resur-rection. This was his crowning miracle, which conquered death and opened the gates of eternal life to all who believed in him. It surpassed any of the Old Testament miracles. A living man might, by divine per-mission, raise a dead one, as Elijah had done. But a dead man as such was ordinarily finished. He could do nothing more. He could not bring himself back to life, unless there was divinity in him as well as humanity.

51

According to the Christians, moreover, when Jesus did rise from the dead, he was not simply a corpse revitalised. He appeared in a mysterious resurrection-body, glorified, strange (since even close followers did not always recognise him at once), and able to pass through closed doors, flit from place to place, and finally 'ascend' leaving this world entirely. The Resurrection was not only a triumph over death, it foreshadowed a new mode of life, a new creation, into which all the blessed would one day enter.

Between the miracles at the beginning and end lies the wonder-working of Jesus's ministry. This is less utterly transcendent, and easier to discuss. The Gospel traditions about it reflect the conflict between what was expected of him, by those who looked to him as Messiah, and what he actually did. It shows in at least one miracle he performs, and also, more clearly, in two he refuses to perform.

In the story of the Temptation in the wilderness, which precedes his public teaching, the Devil urges him to behave as the Messiah should, and work miracles accordingly. He should turn stones into bread. He should fling himself off the roof of the Jerusalem temple, proving who he is by being suspended in the air. Jesus rejects both proposals, and, together with them, the related Messianic motifs – supernatural material welfare as implied in the first, and overawing people by stunts (like a heathen magician) as implied in the second. Satan tempts him again by offering all the kingdoms of the earth. Again he refuses, turning his back on the Messianic power-fantasy itself.

The first miracle which he does perform, shortly afterwards, is described only in *John* 2:1–11. Commentators confess it to be odd, and out of keeping with those that follow. He attends a wedding feast at Cana in Galilee. The wine runs out. His mother draws his attention to the disaster and plainly expects him to take action. At first he rebuffs her, saying his hour has not yet come, but she insists. He tells the servants to fill six big jars with water, and the water is then found to be wine. The quantity is absurd – well over a hundred gallons, involving a long, conspicuous, largely pointless process of fetching from the well. Obviously more is intended than a mere refill. The key to the story is thought to lie in the prophecy of a Messianic banquet, when the Messiah would feast his followers. A huge superabundance of wine is to reveal who Jesus is. He, however, fresh from his encounter with Satan, is unwilling to conform to the image he has just rejected. Turning water into wine, after all, is very like turning stones into bread. He only complies under pressure from his mother (a compliance destined to have momentous results).

After this, impartial reading hints at a cooling of relations between Jesus and most of his kinsfolk. In *Mark* 3:21 they try to put him under restraint as insane. The miracle-stories portray him behaving in a manner likely to excite, but also to bewilder and disappoint.

Few of his feats are even extraordinary in the sense of mere spectacle. They have a moral atmosphere not previously foreseen. Even when he feeds five thousand with a few loaves and fishes, it is not a thaumaturgic lunch-party but an act of compassion. Even when he walks on water, he does not do it in daylight to amaze the crowds, he does it at night and comes to help his disciples in their boat. Most of the miracles are not like these in any case. They are works of healing, bodily or mental – the curing of diseases, the casting-out of demons from crazed victims – and they go with Jesus's teaching as demonstrations of divine love and forgiveness, of the power of good to overcome evil, of the promise of a transmuted life. They point beyond themselves, sometimes towards specific new attitudes. The stress on healing itself defies the ethical norms of the time. Pagans tended to despise the sick; Asclepius, as a god who cared for them, was exceptional. Many Jews were crueller still, regarding illness as a divine punishment for sin. Christ's healing acts imply not only a new sympathy for sufferers, but the lifting of a burden of guilt.

53

Even if these miracles are mythology only, they are still the mythology of a new vision, not of mere wizardry. The Gospel writers seldom refer to them with words suggesting primarily astonishment. The Greek *thaumasion*, meaning an event which is marvelled at, occurs only once (*Matthew* 21:15). *Teras*, meaning a portent, is not a popular word either, and is never used alone to refer to Christ's miracles. The favoured Gospel terms for them are *semeion*, 'sign', and *dunamis*, 'power' or 'act of power'.

Attempts have been made to classify them. C.S. Lewis suggested six headings – fertility, healing, destruction, dominion over the inorganic, reversal, and perfection or glorification. The turning of water into wine, and the multiplication of loaves and fishes, would count as 'fertility'. 'Healing' speaks for itself: Jesus cures leprosy, paralysis and other ills, and restores sanity by exorcism. 'Destruction' is uncommon, but it occurs with a fig-tree which he condemns as barren and causes to wither (*Matthew* 21:18–20) – a story which may symbolise his censure of the Jewish establishment, with its sterile fetish of The Law. 'Dominion over the inorganic' includes controlling the weather (*Mark* 4:37–9) and walking on the sea. 'Reversal' means chiefly restoring the dead to life, as in the case of Lazarus (*John* 11), where a natural process is made to go the opposite way, with a foretaste of a changed creation when all the dead will awaken. 'Perfection or glorification' applies mainly to the resurrection of Christ himself, the new life made momentarily visible.

The Gospel writers certainly intend their readers to think that most of Christ's miracles did literally occur, and were literally miraculous. The early Christians certainly believed that they did, and were. However, an exclusive stress on the question 'What really happened?' is one-sided and misleading. The question 'What are the stories really about?' is also important, and often more so. Some of them, like the fig-tree incident, may actually be meant as allegorical fables. Some may be 'special effects' rather than literal facts – products of a way of putting things which is ancient and oriental rather than modern and western. That applies to several miracles which are signs accompanying Christ rather than direct works of his, such as the bizarre outbreak of apparitions at the time of his death (*Matthew* 27:52–3): 'The tombs also were opened, and many bodies of the saints which had fallen asleep were raised, and coming out of the tombs after his resurrection they went into the holy city and appeared to many.' Here perhaps is an echo of the Roman traditions, used by Shakespeare, of spectral portents at Julius Caesar's passing.

All the same we should be cautious of too much watering-down, too frequent resort to the explanation that 'the writer couldn't mean that this really happened, it's just a symbol or an embellishment'. The literal meaning is nearly always to be preferred as the writer's intention, whether or not we accept it as historical truth. Moreover, events which we would swear were 'symbols' or 'embellishments', if they appeared in an ancient book, do sometimes happen. When we read of darkness overspreading the land at the crucifixion, it is easy to assume that this is pure fantasy or allegory, because nature doesn't correlate with human affairs. Yet at the Vatican Council of 1870, when the bishops voted on papal infallibility, the sunshine of the Roman summer abruptly broke, and a terrific downpour burst on the city. The prelates recorded their 'ayes' one by one in semi-darkness, to an accompaniment of flashes of lightning and peals of thunder. Some observers said God was showing his anger at the impiety of declaring the Pope infallible. Others said Satan was showing his, at a vote which strengthened his chief earthly opponent. The meaning, if any, may be doubtful. The fact is not. It was reported in *The Times*.

However we choose to view these miracles, one thing is certain. They are not presented as arbitrary conjuring tricks, 'proofs' of a mission which would be the same without them. Purely as proofs, indeed, most of them would be dubious even if they happened just as described. There would always be loopholes, and people unwilling to be convinced would always find them. Christ himself disavows the notion of persuasion by miracle. In his parable of the rich man and the beggar Lazarus (*Luke* 16:19–31), he imagines the rich man, tormented in Hades, pleading with Abraham to send the deceased Lazarus back to earth, to warn his brothers of the damnation in store for them. He pleads in vain.

> Abraham said, 'They have Moses and the prophets; let them hear them.' And he said, 'No, father Abraham; but if some one goes to them from the dead, they will repent.' He said to him, 'If they do not hear Moses and the prophets, neither will they be convinced if some one should rise from the dead.'

In the Church's early years the miracles, generally speaking, were not stressed as proving anything by their miraculousness as such. Nor do we hear of many Gentiles being converted by reports of them. The most usual pagan response would not have been to disbelieve, but to ask 'So what?' No doubt they were out of the ordinary, but the Roman world was full of alleged wonder-workers, and it took thoughtful scrutiny to see the difference. Moreover, evil spirits could do surprising things too. The impressiveness of the acts of Christ, when it was acknowledged, did not depend simply on their being extraordinary but on their having that moral quality, that atmosphere, that coherent message, which made them unique. Something higher than humanity, higher than wizardry, shone through them. In making that point, Christians were on firm ground. Pagan wonder-working, as a rule, was scrappy and aimless. The classical world produced only one book which may have been meant as a rival Gospel setting up a rival figure to Christ, the romanticised life of a philosopher named Apollonius, written by Philostratus in the third century. It is quite remarkable how feeble, disconnected

56

and pointless the marvels in that story are. One would have expected an educated pagan to do better.

Today, in the light of critical scholarship and modern knowledge of mind–body relationships, the efficacy of the miracles as direct proof is smaller still. A sceptic can argue, 'Very likely they're only legends anyhow. But if they happened, well, maybe Jesus just had a healing gift ... or maybe the witnesses didn't understand what they saw' ... or this, or that. At the utmost the miracles can prove no more in themselves than that a superhuman power was at work. It may or may not have been divine in the Christian sense. It may or may not have been genuinely good. Like our forebears, if not for quite the same reasons, we must accept that the only way to handle these marvels is to go beyond their marvellousness.

Once more, the main point of Christ's miracles lies in their meaning, in what they are held to reveal about him, and, through him, about God. They are woven so closely into the fabric that they cannot be unpicked. In a sense the entire story of Christ is about a single supreme miracle, the Incarnation itself, God-made-man. All his miracles in detail follow on from this, and are, so to speak, contained in it. Since the Incarnation, if it happened at all, was unique in history, it is doubtful how far we can apply ordinary canons of criticism. There is nothing else enough like it to justify drawing comparisons and inferences.

The obvious comment is: 'Then it's simply a matter of faith, not discussion. You believe or you don't. The Christian (the traditional Christian, at any rate) buys the whole package and places it outside rational argument. Perhaps he can't be refuted, but there is no reason why anybody else should agree with him.' However, it is not quite so simple. There is a problem here, already foreshadowed, which cannot be banished by denial alone. If you reject the Christian's package, he can fairly ask what alternative package you offer to account for the facts. After all, the Church did come into being as a

57

matter of history, claiming that it began because of such-and-such events which actually happened, including the miracles. If its own account of its origins is false, then what is the truth, how did it originate? In particular, can you get rid of the miraculous and still explain all the facts?

Most people assume that this can be done. We can prune it all away and be left with a purely human 'historical Jesus', who was built up into a divine Messiah by legend; or perhaps with a 'Christ-myth', an edifying fable about a saviour who never existed. Without going into the complexities that surround this issue, it is worth remarking that in spite of the hatred which the early Christians aroused, we never hear of their story being refuted or even contradicted, or of any contemporary, Jewish or Roman, retorting to them with a hostile Truth about Jesus. Considering how welcome this would have been to the authorities, the Christians' story cannot have been as palpably false as many modern authors would like to suggest. It is also worth remarking that if the Gospels are largely fiction, concocted to build up Jesus as the Messiah, we have to ask why the writers made him *un*like the Messiah, refusing to work the sort of miracles that were expected, and eschewing earthly power. Every critical attempt at explaining-away comes up against the obvious presence of stubborn facts, which neither the Christians nor their enemies could avoid.

There is a further reflection, which may be more interesting, and is certainly more mystifying. For a century and a half, a whole series of learned critics, from David Strauss and Ernest Renan onwards, have assumed that 'miracles don't happen' and approached the Gospels with that dogma in mind, contriving alternative Lives of Jesus. They have all tried to carry out the pruning process and get down to a non-miraculous person, or to a myth invented by non-miraculous persons. And they have come up with a long parade of contradictory answers. They make out Jesus to have been simply a

58

healer, or an exorcist, or a moralist; to have been a pacifist, a socialist, a prophet of doomsday, an Essene Teacher of Righteousness, a Jewish Nationalist, a lunatic; a sun-myth, a vegetation-myth, a hallucinogenic mushroom. Sometimes a consensus 'historical Jesus' emerges dimly from the debate and lasts a few years, but always the next fashion in criticism replaces him with another. Furthermore not one of these reduced figures, or fables, could have had that overwhelming impact without which the entire history makes no sense. Not one could account for the Church having established itself at all. Any of them might have inspired a minor cult, none could have inspired the institution that came into existence.

So the question 'If not this, then what?' is unanswered. The only safe conclusion is that the reality was richer and more mysterious than its would-be analysts have cared to admit. Of course their work has been important. They have made discoveries of immense value in understanding the Gospels. What they have failed to do, with all the vast and ever-growing resources of scholarship, is to provide a story that supersedes them, cutting out the supernatural and leaving a residual Jesus who carries conviction.

Logic drives us, by default, to take the picture of Christ as a whole – miracles and all – and construe it as best we can. Wrangling in detail over the value of the testimony, and whether the Gospels do or do not give us eye-witness reports, is rather old-fashioned and bound to be inconclusive. Some of the miracles can be rationalised. Some can be treated as symbolic. Some can be reduced to a way-of-putting-things which is not ours. But it is futile to discard them as legend. Generations of scholars have tried it, and ended up in hopeless confusion over the nature of what is left. The package is a package. Either we accept it in substance and believe in Christ's miracles, or we confront the question 'If not this, then what?' and the fact that, up to now, no one has offered a rational alternative that survives scrutiny and accounts for the historical sequel. Either the thing happened more or less as the Church concluded, or something else happened which remains utterly mysterious.

In the twentieth century the question 'If not this, then what?' has taken a strange incidental turn, outside the debate about the Gospels themselves. It has posed a challenge over one of the best-known sacred relics, the Holy Shroud of Turin. Some have claimed that this is physical evidence for the greatest of Jesus's miracles, the Resurrection.

The Holy Shroud is kept in a chest in Turin Cathedral and only very rarely exposed to view. It is a wide strip of linen thirteen feet long, very worn and undoubtedly very old. Along its length are two brownish stains which dimly sketch a human figure, front view and back view. These are said to be marks made by the body of Christ. Supposedly, after crucifixion, he was laid on the Shroud face up with his feet near one end. The other end was then lifted, and carried over his head down to his feet, sandwiching the body, which stained the cloth above and below. Inside the brown markings are spots of red. These are said to be blood.

Such a relic, on the face of it, is most unlikely to be authentic. The Shroud's proved history only goes back to the fourteenth century, when it was at Lirey, near Troyes, in France. There are grounds for thinking that it was once at Constantinople and was brought home by a crusader. However, the record before the Crusades is a near-blank. Authentication in that sense is wholly lacking. The problem of the Shroud is not documentary but visual.

In 1898 it was photographed for the first time, with unexpected results. The negative, transposing the light and dark areas, turned the long brown stains into a double image (front and back) of a tall man, with a sad, noble, bearded face. Whatever cause had created this image was clearly more subtle and interesting than simple contact with a body. If the cloth had been pressed down and pushed in, to follow the body's contours, any prints made by staining would have been distorted. But there was no distortion. If it had lain lightly, the upper stain, corresponding to the front view including the face, would have had blank patches where the cloth did not touch. But it seemed to be complete.

When the photograph was published, Paul Vignon, a lecturer at the Sorbonne in Paris, boldly suggested that the Shroud was genuine and that the markings were of chemical origin. The sweat on the corpse would, he claimed, have reacted with the herbs used in burial to release vapour capable of staining the fabric. A respected biologist, Yves Delage, presented this theory in a paper read to the French Academy of Sciences. As Delage was an agnostic, with no religious axe to grind, his paper attracted wide attention. Debate over the Shroud has gone on sporadically ever since. Doctors have declared that the alleged bloodstains, and other traces of physical damage, agree with what could be expected if the man in the Shroud had endured the blows, scourging and crowning with thorns described in scripture. Moreover, there are details which are right, but at odds with the conventional ideas which a fabricator would have followed. For instance, if a man were crucified without adequate suppport for his body weight, the nails would need to be driven through his wrists, because in the hands the flesh would tear; and one side-effect would be a reflex making the thumbs turn inwards. Here the Shroud figure diverges correctly from the imagination of artists. The nail-marks are in the wrists, and the thumbs turn inwards.

Hence, the natural theory of a fake has difficulties to overcome. Its chief advocate, a priest named Ulysse Chevalier, played what he thought a trump card by unearthing a statement made by a bishop of Troyes in 1389. The bishop said that the Shroud (then in his diocese) was a painting, and the painter had confessed. Common sense would accept that statement as final. The trouble is that it can hardly apply to the Shroud

61

now at Turin, though somebody may have made a copy. The Turin picture is not a coating as paint would be, it is right in the fabric. No medieval paint would have stained the cloth in that way. Even if an artist had happened to invent water-colours, they would have spread along the threads and made a faulty outline. Also there is the weird fact of the picture being a negative. No known process of fading could have done this. To paint it negative in the first place would have been very difficult – almost impossible without photography as a guide – and entirely pointless, unlikely to occur to a faker who could not foresee how the camera would one day reveal his work. Further, it is doubtful whether a fourteenth-century artist could have done anything so exact and vivid, and it is almost certain that no such artist could have got the physical damage right. The knowledge did not exist.

So the fraud theory runs into a blind alley. But so, alas, does the theory of the Shroud's genuineness, as stated by the scientists. Vignon never managed to make a vapour-print such as he supposed the picture of Christ to be. Experiments along other lines have failed equally. Images have been formed by vapour and other suggested means, but never with the same characteristics. While the Shroud stains could not apparently have been painted, they would not have been made by a corpse either, through any natural process yet hit upon.

Is the deadlock complete? Not quite, but the implications of the one known solution might be thought disquieting. This is my own single contribution to the study of the miraculous. My experiment consisted in heating a brass ornament with a design in relief, and laying a white handkerchief for an instant on the hot metal. The result was an image formed by scorching, which had the same qualities as those on the Shroud. To the eyes it was a brown stain of unequal darkness. In photographic negative it was a good reproduction of the design, with an effect of depth.

A human body, even a living one, could never make a

scorch-picture like this in the normal course of events. It is nowhere near hot enough. But according to the Gospels, the body of Christ did not follow the normal course of events. In some supernatural manner it returned to life. Who can say what would happen in such a case? A sudden burst of radiation, perhaps – radiation capable of making a picture, like the one scorched by heat into the handkerchief? We can say that the Shroud might have become as it is, if it once enwrapped a crucified corpse to which something extraordinary happened. The Resurrection?

This is a view of the Shroud which, over the years, has achieved some acceptance. It seems far-fetched. But we have no plausible alternative. Nobody, I repeat, has shown how a corpse could have made this imprint without the 'something extraordinary'. It is futile to suggest that the Shroud was used to wrap a crucified man but that he was not Jesus. If he simply died and was buried, he would not have marked it thus. As for faking, the artistic and anatomical quality seem out of the question for the fourteenth century. In any case, how was the faking done? Even if it had occurred to some eccentric artist to make a life-size metal relief and use my scorch technique, I do not believe he could have applied it to such a large cloth. The Shroud is no handkerchief. It would have flapped and sagged and touched the metal unevenly, probably burning through in some places before it met the surface in others.

As with the Gospel story itself, the present choice with the Holy Shroud of Turin is between the miraculous and the incomprehensible. The miraculous is an answer of sorts. If not this, then what?

Judaism, let us recall, had evolved the idea of a special relationship with God. Christianity carried it on and made it more concrete. Since Christ *was* God, his apostles stood in such a relationship. In the book of *Acts* we are told of miracles happening for them too, after he had gone. These are like his own. They are, in

63

fact, a continuation of his, an assurance of the unbroken divine presence. Peter and his colleagues heal the sick, cast out devils and raise the dead. However, we do not hear of any more miracles suggesting mastery of inanimate nature, such as walking on water.

In a world where professed magicians abounded, Christian wonder-working, real or reputed, was open to a construction that devalued it. Was it merely a superior magic? *Acts* 8:9–24 portrays Peter clashing on that issue with Simon Magus. Simon is known from other sources. He was a magician of high standing, the founder of a sect of his own which became the source of others, the so-called Gnostic systems. It appears that he submitted to Christian baptism and was impressed by the miracles, but thought they were performed through an occult power, which could be conferred on people at will and used at will. He approached Peter and John offering payment for it, with a view to building up his own coterie of miracle-workers. Peter, however, sternly refused. 'Your silver perish with you, because you thought you could obtain the gift of God with money!' Simon was shaken and went away. Here the idea of magic is disavowed. Whatever happens is God's gift, not the result of a technique, to be bought and sold as a commodity.

A hostile Jewish account of Jesus gives another opinion. This book is fiction, written centuries afterwards and without value as history. Still it is interesting for what it covertly concedes. It makes out that Jesus was a sorcerer, and that the miracles were done by black arts. The noteworthy point is that the author does not deny them, as an anti-Christian would today. The tradition of Jesus's having worked them must have been too strong to dismiss, even among the Church's opponents.

That being so, his followers' stories of more or less unlimited marvels, not only among the New Testament characters but among their successors, could always impress an audience. They bulk larger in the Church's progress after the first couple of centuries than they do in the early period. With the waning of Rome and the advance of superstition, Christian marvels from Jesus onward acquire that aura of 'proof' which they were not originally seen as possessing – not, at least, to anything like the same extent. A modern historian has remarked (perhaps a shade unfairly) that to judge from the writings of the Venerable Bede, the Anglo-Saxons were converted by a series of conjuring tricks.

Catholic Christianity went on associating miracles with its saints, right through to the Reformation and after. For Protestants these later wonders presented a problem. Having broken away on the ground that the Church was corrupt, and had become so quite early in its career, they could not very well admit them. Popish miracles implied that the Whore of Babylon had not forfeited God's approval as the Protestants claimed. They therefore tried to argue that the saints' miracles, which were false, could be distinguished from the scriptural miracles, which were true. This position proved hard to maintain. As bolder critics presently pointed out, the arguments that were used against the false ones could also be used against the true ones, discrediting Christianity altogether. Nor could Protestants agree on where to draw the line. While some stood firm in denying miracles after the apostolic age, others wavered, allowing that they went on for two, three, or four centuries before dying out. In the absence of an 'anti' consensus, Catholics simply repeated that they never ceased at all.

General recognition since the eighteenth century that most miracle-stories are legend has not affected Rome's basic position. In the Catholic context miracles can still happen. It is claimed in fact that they do. We shall see that the most conspicuous cases in recent years are of this kind. As to whether there have ever been Protestant miracles, opinions differ. John Wesley believed that he had witnessed inexplicable cures due to prayer, but he never laid much stress on them.

The biographies, or pseudo-biographies, of Catholic saints include many miracles like those of the apostles –

healing, exorcism and so forth – with occasional direct echoes of Christ, such as feeding a crowd with a little bread (told in near-modern times of the Italian youth worker St John Bosco). They also include pure fairy-tale incidents, as when a missionary crosses the sea on a floating altar, or a monk hangs his cloak on a sunbeam. They further include feats that might be described as paranormal: thought-reading, for instance, and manifestations such as appearing in visions and bilocating – that is, being in two places at once, Some of the tales in this latter class are truly spectacular. In 1620–3 Maria d'Agreda, a Spanish nun, was preaching to the Indians of New Mexico while living uninterruptedly in her convent. (Maria has never actually been canonised, but her mission is an essentially saintly performance.)

The fairy-tale incidents are Christian folklore, often adapted from pre-Christian legend. In general they could be piled up endlessly without adding much to the consideration of miracles. The paranormal feats are best deferred for the moment. Some of them, if hardly Sister Maria's, deserve to be taken seriously, but as a class they fall into place in another context. More interesting at this point, and more strictly apposite, is a rather un-scriptural type of miracle, which reinforces the Christian stress on the hand of God, as distinct from the will of man. This is the miracle which is done not *by* or *through* the saint but *for* him, without any intent of his own, perhaps without his being aware of it, as a token of his special relationship with God. Such miracles have a kind of antecedent in Pentecost (*Acts* 2:1–4), when the Holy Spirit descended on the apostles in tongues of fire, and inspired them to speak in different languages. Pentecost, however, was functional, charging them with their mission. The tokens given to the saints are that and no more.

Miracles of levitation belong in this class. The holy men and women of Christendom are not, of course, the only ones who rise from the ground. Indian yogis are said to do the same. But whereas the yogis claim to do it

66

themselves, by concentration of thought, the saints are taken up in the air by what seems celestial caprice. They make no conscious effort, and would have no notion how to go about it if they wanted to.

Levitation is not reported of very many. The favoured few, however, include several of great distinction, spiritually and intellectually. Among them are the philosopher St Thomas Aquinas, the religious foundress and author St Teresa of Avila, and her friend the poet-mystic St John of the Cross. As a rule the thing is said to happen in moments of ecstasy, and to be quiet and unspectacular, an upward movement of a few inches. However, the best attested case is that of an obscure Italian friar, whose flights were of much more than a few inches, and were confirmed by so many eye-witnesses, including Protestants, that historians outside the Church have been disposed to believe in them. This story is so baffling that the only thing to do with it is to sum it up and pass on.

St Joseph of Cupertino was born in 1603. As a boy he was stupid and dreamy. Admitted to a Franciscan community as a stable-hand, he pulled himself together somewhat, and was ordained priest at twenty-two. One day after saying Mass, he floated upwards and found himself standing on the altar. Several more such flights induced his superiors to send him to Pope Urban VIII for examination. He levitated in front of the Pope. Over the ensuing years his gift, if it can be called so, came and went, but tended on the whole to establish itself. The flights grew longer.

They were always triggered by an impulse of joy, not necessarily religious. Music or colour could be enough. Joseph flew when shepherds played their pipes in the church at Christmas. He flew when a brother monk remarked on the beauty of the sky. In church he was known to travel fifteen yards, and the monk's comment on the sky propelled him to the top of a tree. Sometimes the flight was prefaced by an impromptu dance, but there is no evidence that this was a conscious warming-up, or that Joseph had mediumistic powers or anything of that kind. He gave the impression of being a holy innocent, a beloved simpleton. He does appear to have had some control over his flying when it took place, and to have shown a sense of humour. On one occasion he startled a Spanish dignitary and his wife by soaring over their heads. On others he took passengers with him, such as a nobleman in a fit of insanity, whom he cured by carrying aloft on a quarter-hour hover. Witnesses of Joseph's ascents ran into hundreds. Among them was the future mathematician and philosopher Leibniz. A Lutheran duke with whom he was travelling was converted to Catholicism by the sight of Joseph raised off the floor, without change of posture, as he knelt before the altar.

So much for the arch-levitator. Another such miracle of divine blessing is stigmatisation, the imprinting of wounds in the hands and feet recalling those of Christ, sometimes with others in the body and head, corresponding to the spear-thrust (*John* 19:34) and the crown of thorns. It may be significant that stigmatics have received the hand-wounds as they doubtless pictured them, in the palms, not as they probably were, in the wrists. The first on record is no less a person than St Francis of Assisi. In 1224 Francis had a vision of a crucified seraph, and afterwards found his own hands and feet to be pierced. Since then, over three hundred cases have been asserted. Most of them are doubtful, and most of the few good ones may have been psychosomatic. In 1932 an Austrian doctor, Adolph Lechler, harmlessly stigmatised a woman patient by hypnotic suggestion, and then reversed the process.

This patient, however, was under treatment for hysteria, and hysteria was certainly not present in the most famous modern case. Padre Pio (Pio Forgione), an Italian friar like Joseph of Cupertino, died in 1968 after a long, sane and beneficent life, during which doctors of various persuasions studied his stigmata without fixing on a natural cause for them. A hard-working, conscientious man of peasant stock, Pio's first eleven years in his monastery went by without his seeming to be remarkable, except in one respect. When he was ill, his temperature rose so high that it broke a clinical thermometer, and was found to be 45°C – that is, 112°F. On September 20th, 1915, he complained of crippling pains in his hands, feet and side. Thereafter he was seldom at complete physical ease. Three years later he collapsed at prayer, in the presence of other members of his community. Wounds, bleeding profusely, appeared in the places where he had felt the pain.

His stigmata remained on him for the rest of his life. Bandages kept the bleeding under control. He was reluctant to unwind them even for a brief scrutiny, having no wish to be the focus of a personality cult. Doctors who did examine the wounds found them puzzling, though some proposed a rare kind of auto-suggestion.

He became renowned as a spiritual adviser, a very kind and perceptive one, with no hint of unbalance about him. Miraculous cures were reported among the people who came to him. Two who had defective eyes, medically incapable of sight, did see after visiting Padre Pio. Many who made confessions to him declared that he was a thought-reader and knew what they were going to tell him before they spoke. He was also credited with clairvoyance, and with bilocation. Even before his visible wounding he is said to have appeared to the Italian General Cadorna and dissuaded him from shooting himself after a defeat. Cadorna did not know the monk whom he saw and heard in his tent, but later, at a church where Padre Pio was saying mass, he recognised him. On the way back from the altar Pio came over to him and whispered: 'You had a lucky escape, my friend.'

Levitation and stigmatisation are the chief types of miracle in which the holy person is a passive recipient of divine power. Other symptoms of holiness on the same lines are an almost-incredible body heat, as with Padre Pio, and a subtle fragrance, also attributed to him as to a number of others. Some holy persons are alleged to have survived for an amazing time with little or no food. Also, when someone of reputed sanctity is exhumed long after death, the body is apt to be incorrupt. This of course is known to occur with non-saints (I remember having read that the champion liar Baron Munchausen was very slow to decay), but with those beloved of the Church it seems to be more frequent, and is taken into account in proceedings for their canonisation.

When considering the array of saintly miracles, both active and passive, Catholics of the wiser sort are careful to keep the proper distinctions in view. However superstition may blur the issue, they never pretend that a saint can cause miracles by taking thought, or devise a technique for doing them, or teach anyone else to do them. Nor could a human being force God's hand by trying to *become* a saint – by being rigidly virtuous, or cultivating total faith.

On this last point, much unnecessary grief has been caused (perhaps more among Protestants than Catholics) by a too-literal reading of Christ's saying in *Matthew* 17:20: 'If you have faith as a grain of mustard seed, you will say to this mountain, "Move from here to there", and it will move; and nothing will be impossible to you.' These words are surely figurative. They have often been taken, however, as meaning that faith is a magic power which works automatically, so that anyone with enough of it could do miracles at will, like Wells's Mr Fotheringay. This is a stupid thing to suggest, and also cruel, because of what it implies if you feel confident of your faith and then a miracle fails to happen. In Somerset Maugham's novel *Of Human Bondage*, a lame boy is encouraged to think that if he has enough faith his lameness will be cured. When it is not, the only comment offered by his clergyman mentor is that his faith could not have been sufficient. In view of the importance of faith for salvation, such a verdict can push an impressionable Christian towards despair, or towards rejection of his religion for the wrong reasons.

The idea is not only mistaken but gravely false in its

70

emphasis. The greater minds of the Church, Teresa of Avila for instance, take a view of these matters which is shared by their counterparts in the East. Miracles are worked, yes, through holy persons and for them. When they happen they are signs of spiritual progress. They may also do good to others, by curing disease or lifting the spirits. In themselves, however, they do not matter very much. A holy man who stressed his own miracles would probably be going astray. Anyone who tried to copy the saints in the hope of winning supernatural favours would be going astray more drastically.

Making too much of miracles also involves the hazard of being deluded by bogus ones. These, according to Catholic tradition, include not only the endless deceptions and self-deceptions of Christians, but also seductive wonder-working by evil agencies. With, for example, the phenomena of spiritualism, such as the levitations and table-turnings of the famous Victorian medium Daniel Home, the Catholic explanation used to be (and in some quarters, still is) that they are caused by devils with intent to deceive. Devils cannot work genuine miracles, but they have a limited paranormal power, like that of the black magicians with whom they ally themselves. They can do startling things. They can seem to do others which are more startling, though only by cheating: thus, their cures are not real cures.

A diabolic trick may look like a divine miracle, in itself and at the time. When Daniel Home floated out of the window – as witnesses assure us he did – the event was not very different, on the face of it, from the flights of St Joseph of Cupertino. To tell a true miracle from a false one, there is need for appraisal of the background, of the people concerned, of the moral atmosphere, of the implications and consequences. Home himself briefly managed such an appraisal, or thought he did, and the result was that he repudiated his own feats and turned Catholic, though it did not last. His steadfast admirers, uncritically impressed by the marvels of mediumship, were (on a Catholic reading) tricked into

unhealthy delusions by malign spirits making use of
him.

Since the saints are close to God, he goes on acting
through them and with them after their death. They are
in his presence in heaven, and divine power responds to
their petitions. Christians began praying to the martyrs
about the third century AD, perhaps earlier. The scriptural justification for this was *Revelation* 6:9–11, a passage which portrays those who had died for the Faith as
aware in heaven of the sufferings of Christians on earth,
and calling for divine judgment on Roman persecutors.

When Christianity became the Empire's religion,
there were no more martyrs. The Church gradually admitted the cult of other saints. Presently heaven was not
only in communication with earth through many ap-
proved channels, but departmentalised like the old
pagan pantheon. Individual saints became the patrons
of countries (St George for England), of occupations (St
Crispin for shoemakers), and of many other branches of
life. Those that have survived recent Vatican purges still
take an interest in special ailments (you pray to St Blaise
when you have trouble with your throat), or assist in
special difficulties (you pray to St Anthony when you
have lost something). The saints' help has often been
associated with their shrines. It may be given in response to a pilgrim's prayer on the spot, or the favoured
person may make a pilgrimage afterwards in thanksgiving, like Chaucer's company going to the shrine of
Thomas à Becket at Canterbury.

The saints have powers in heaven which are above
those of earthly humanity, and they can act in various
ways. Their help occasionally comes in the shape of
outright miracles worked at their request. This aspect of
the miraculous is important, because the Church has
tended to take the view that there is no other proof of
anyone actually having been a saint. If he was, he is in
heaven now, and it is right to venerate him and pray to
him. But the only evidence that can make us sure of his

72

whereabouts is the working of miracles through his intercession.

They therefore play a crucial role in canonisation. This means official recognition that somebody really is a saint, and that a cult of him can be permitted. It does not happen casually or overnight. There has to be a demand first, which may take years, even centuries, to build up. When Rome is convinced that many of the faithful want this person to be 'raised to the altars of the Church', as the phrase goes, certain steps are taken. One is a detailed probing of all that is on record about the candidate. Another is the launching of a provisional and partial cult. Catholics are allowed, sometimes encouraged, to pray together for miracles through the candidate's intercession. In theory, at least two must occur. If they do he may progress through beatification, an interim step, to full canonisation. None of this is at all certain. Sometimes his cause simply peters out. Sometimes it goes only a part of the way. Quite a number of the beatified have never been canonised and are therefore known as 'Blessed So-and-so', not 'Saint'.

Prayer for a miracle may be specific. When someone is desperately ill, Catholics may pray for that person to be cured through the candidate's intercession. This happened in 1976 with the canonisation of the Scottish martyr John Ogilvy. The rules for deciding when a cure can count as miraculous were laid down in the eighteenth century by Benedict XIV, a pope with scientific interests. As a precaution against hasty claims, he made it clear that Rome would not entertain the case for a miracle if a natural explanation could be arrived at. In the then state of medical knowledge the hindrance was not severe. However, he added seven positive conditions which still apply, and, now as then, would make canonisation very rare indeed if they were all strictly adhered to with every candidate. They are:

1. That the illness should be serious, and impossible, or at least very difficult, to cure.

73

2. That the illness should not be on the decline or of such a nature that it might in any case improve.
3. That no medication should have been given, or if it has been given, that its inefficacy should be clearly established.
4. That the cure should be sudden, instantaneous.
5. That the cure should be complete.
6. That the cure should not correspond to a crisis in the illness brought about by natural causes.
7. That after the cure there should be no recurrence of the illness in question.

Cures which may be judged to meet these requirements are known to happen. In the John Ogilvy process, a man seemingly within hours of dying from cancer suddenly recovered. But Pope Benedict's conditions make a miracle so hard to establish that in practice they have sometimes been stretched a little.

Besides personal intervention from heaven, a saint may still be present on earth through his relics. Christians inherited this idea from the Greeks, whose temples enshrined the alleged bones of heroes, and possessions of theirs such as weapons and musical instruments. Christian relics, however, were more active in their properties.

It is uncertain how early they began to be revered as more than mementoes. When Polycarp of Smyrna was burnt at the stake in 156, his disciples gathered up his bones and preserved them. By the fourth century, small fragments of the holy dead were being hoarded in special caskets called reliquaries. In 304 we hear of bystanders dipping pieces of linen in a martyr's blood and keeping them as heirlooms. Soon afterwards not only the remains of the saints themselves, but objects even tenuously connected with them (such as garments they wore and chairs they sat in) are spoken of as occasions for divine wonder-working. Early in the fifth century a point has been reached where St Augustine can refer to miracles performed by flowers which have touched a reliquary, by oil from the lamps in a martyr's church, by soil from the Holy Land. Scriptural warrant for the efficacy of relics is slight, but it exists. In *II Kings* 13:21 a dead man revives upon contact with the bones of the prophet Elisha. In *Acts* 19:11–12 the sick are healed even during Paul's lifetime by cloths which he has touched.

The huge and absurd proliferation of relics in later times is beside the point here. It includes attempts to claim various objects as relics of characters in the Bible itself; among these, the Holy Shroud is genuinely remarkable and most of the others are absurd. As with canonisation, miracles play a part in the growth of the cult of relics in general. For many centuries, if a question arose as to whether a relic was authentic, there was only one accepted test. Did it work miracles? If it did, it was judged to be truly a portion or possession of the saint it was alleged to belong to, and a channel for his action in earthly affairs. Since the miracles worked by relics were seldom subjected to critical scrutiny themselves, wishful thinking produced them in swarms and thereby authenticated many relics which had no right to credence.

With two of the most famous, which continue to attract crowds, miracle-working is the essence of the story. A church at Loreto near Ancona in Italy contains the Santa Casa or Holy House, which is said to be the actual, literal dwelling of the Virgin Mary in Nazareth. Its transportation from Galilee was not the work of human hands but of God himself, and it was in three stages. In 1291, the house (still intact after thirteen centuries) left its foundations and flew through space to Fiume on the Adriatic. Three years later it moved to Recanati. Shortly after that it reached its final resting-place on a plot of ground belonging to a Lady Lauretta, and the town of Loreto grew around it. While the major miracle is assigned to a distant past, the Holy House has proved itself by working many lesser ones since.

The case is somewhat different with that other renowned relic, the blood of St Januarius. Here the central marvel is not a once-for-all event in the past but a repeated happening in the present. Januarius, martyred in 305, is the patron saint of Naples. At Naples Cathedral, on certain holy days, a large image of him is enthroned before the congregation. The Bishop holds up a glass vial with two handles. In it can be seen a dark substance which is said to be congealed blood of the saint. The Bishop shakes it and swings it about; the people pray; and after a while, usually but not always, the dark stuff apparently liquefies. Failure to do so is a bad omen for the city. In 1977 the liquefaction was televised at fairly close quarters, though anyone who cared to think that it was a trick, based on a hollow handle with liquid inside, saw nothing to prove otherwise.

St Januarius's public performance has survived from the Middle Ages into a more sceptical era. Many other marvels have not. The full-blown cult of the saints in medieval Christendom had much about it that was corrupt, foolish, pathetic. It also had much that was moving and endearing, with a deep sense of human community, a fellowship of the living and dead. But most of the homage paid to Saints This and That, however ardent, was overshadowed by the cult of another departed being – as indeed it was at Loreto. In this, the Christian saga of the miraculous rose to a second peak. Through it, a train of events began which put miracles in a fresh light and has not yet reached its term.

4

The Lady Whom God Obeys

As I have said in another place, the cult of the Blessed
Virgin is the most impressive of all psychological case-
histories. It is much more, of course. But to consider
Mary and the Catholic vision of her is to discern Christianity changing course, and, in the process, admitting a
new mode of thought about the miraculous. She who
becomes queen of all the saints is above them in nature
as well as honour. Her cult raises issues which the cult of
the saints in general does not. As will presently appear,
beliefs about Mary and her celestial wonder-working
have an interest outside Catholicism. They offer clues to
phenomena which at first sight seem unrelated.

The origins of devotion to the Mother of Christ are
obscure. Certainly, however, it came in fulfilment of an
ancestral need which the Church up to then had failed to
meet. It will be recalled that male gods rose to ascendancy during the second millennium BC by supplanting
the older divinity of the female. With them came those
autocratic systems of cosmic law that produced the idea
of the exception as a divine monopoly, and therefore the
idea of the miraculous. In the Graeco-Roman world
they reigned throughout the classical era. Early Christianity with its male Saviour and Trinity was a continuation along the same line. But behind the public
paganism of the time, a nostalgia for female divinity,
with its glamour and ambiguity and long-lost hope of
eternal life, had lingered on. At the beginning of the
Christian era, Goddess-figures such as Demeter and Isis
were enjoying a new life in the Mystery cults. These
were not for the masses; they were exclusive and ex-
pensive; but the initiates were people of social standing,
with influence out of proportion to their numbers. At
length, in the worship of Mary, the same ancient and

subversive thing arose more powerfully out of the past and broke into Christianity itself – not the weak, struggling Christianity of the era of persecution, but the triumphant mass creed of the fourth and fifth centuries, established in its supremacy by Christian emperors.

Where did Mary's cult come from? As a New Testament character, she never says or does anything to justify her later glorification in the form it takes. Honest reading rather suggests that her Son became estranged from her, and that the first Christians, except perhaps for John, had no great attachment to her. She is absent from the accounts of the Resurrection, where we would expect to read of Jesus consoling her as he consoles others close to him. If her cult has any historical basis, it may lie partly in unrecorded later events which revived her importance in the eyes of at least some Christians. Catholic doctrine speaks of her Assumption or taking up to heaven. Though this idea cannot be traced earlier than the fifth century, it seems to be grounded on a much older popular belief that she attained some mysterious final glory, and entered immortality as a female counterpart of the deathless Elijah.

Whatever the nature of this belief, it had very little effect on orthodox teaching. For more than three hundred years there is no sign of anyone in the Church regarding the Virgin as a living presence, a being who can be prayed to or who can act in the world. So far as can be made out, she was first worshipped and hailed as Queen of Heaven by a sect of women outside the Church, nicknamed Collyridians. The only churchman who writes about them, a bishop named Epiphanius in the fourth century, treats them with scorn and says 'Let no one worship Mary'. But the devotion was spreading, and despite Epiphanius's attack, it was seeping into the Church itself when he wrote.

The first known mention by a priest, in his official capacity, of prayer to the Virgin as a proper and commendable act, is in a sermon preached at Constantinople by St Gregory of Nazianzus. It can be dated almost precisely to October 379. Gregory tells a story (moral fiction, not history) about Justina, a Christian maiden, who was seized by unholy passion for Cyprian, a pagan. To defeat it she fasted, and disfigured her looks so as to make herself unattractive. Furthermore she begged the Virgin to help her, a virgin in peril. Thereby spiritually sustained, she survived intact. Cyprian was converted by her example.

Marian adoration was gaining ground during the next half-century, and received the Church's approval at the Council of Ephesus in 431. After that its success was immense. Most of the driving force came from the populace, not the clergy. Then as later the creative energy of the cult was democratic, and only the attempts to control and define it were authoritarian. At the outset the main motive was simply the ancestral hunger for female deity. A second reason was that the Trinity seemed to have grown remote, and unhelpful (to put it mildly) in the disasters besetting the Roman world, so that a nearer, maternal protectress was ardently desired.

Of course there had to be adjustments. The Collyridian women had made Mary actually divine. The clerics could not do that. They drew her into their system as Mother of God, a correct if paradoxical title since Jesus *was* God, and placed her in a special position, below the Trinity but above the rest of humanity. A special kind of worship took shape for her. The worship due to God and no other being was called *latria*, the veneration due to the saints was called *dulia*, and the worship – or veneration – of Mary was given the new name of *hyperdulia*, and reserved for her only.

The first recorded Marian miracles occurred in the very place where Gregory told the tale of Justina. His endorsement of the practice of prayer to the Virgin seems to have made a deep impression. Soon afterwards a new church was put up on the site of the building in Constantinople where he preached. Here, according to a historian named Sozomen who wrote during the 440s

79

(within the lifetime of eye-witnesses), marvels began to happen.

> A divine power was there manifested, and was helpful both in waking visions and in dreams, often for the relief of many diseases and for those afflicted by some sudden transmutation in their affairs. The power was attributed to Mary, the Mother of God, the holy Virgin, for she does manifest herself in this way.

'She does manifest herself in this way' – in the 440s, clearly, a Marian norm was already recognised. Not that the miracle-pattern we have been studying was replaced in Christian minds, then or later. Christians continued to believe that the natural order was derived from God, and that although exceptions did occur, it was God himself who injected them into it. No other being had the power; the utmost that might be said was that God sometimes chose to do it through a particular person. In that sense alone, a saint, on earth or in heaven, could be a miracle-worker. The case of Mary, however, confronts us with a 'particular person' whose miracles are unique. Reviving, after her fashion, the reign of the Womanly before God's monopoly of exceptions, she subtly modifies that monopoly without directly defying it.

Despite all goddesses in the background, she remains within the limits prescribed and never becomes a goddess herself. Even the extremest Mariolaters confess that she is a created being. It is because she is seen as human, but human in a unique relationship to God, that she has such a fascinating role in the history of miracles, and opens up another way of regarding them.

Many of the Virgin's characteristic feats have their prototype in a single Greek legend. This was already current in the sixth century, perhaps earlier. It has a double claim to attention, since it is the prototype of the Faust legend as well (and Goethe, when his Faust dies and is saved after all, restores Mary to the story).

Theophilus of Adana, it is said, was a Christian who

aspired to a post from which his bishop excluded him. Thwarted beyond endurance, he consulted a Jewish sorcerer. The Jew led him at midnight to an assembly of white-robed figures carrying candles, with the Devil in their midst. Satan demanded that Theophilus sign a pact denying Christ. He did so, and his fortunes improved. But he realised that he was on the road to perdition. His remorse attracted the Virgin's notice and compassion. Not only did she intercede and obtain God's forgiveness, she compelled Satan to disgorge the pact, which returned into Theophilus's hands. He made a public confession and the damning document was burned.

From a strictly Christian point of view, the ethics of this tale are equivocal. Thanks to Mary, Theophilus seems to have it both ways. Yet the wonder she works for him is the pattern for a great many more. The Mary cult which grew up steadily through the Middle Ages was not merely a more opulent version of the cult of the saints. It was a revolt of humanity within the Church's legalistic God-centred scheme. It was a means of getting off the hook, whether through actual miracles or through exceptions of a more general kind.

Obviously it had its financial aspects, and its allure for a celibate clergy seeking sublimation. Feminists may be right when they argue that by steering men's reverence towards an idealised woman on a pedestal, the clergy left them free to go on treating real women with cruelty and contempt. Feminists may also be right when they argue that the stress on a Virgin Mother and female 'purity' was a male-biased condemnation of complete womanhood. All these factors were doubtless present, yet they did not exhaust the cult's contents, because something stronger than the priesthood – female divinity in fact – was constantly breaking through. It expressed itself in a human figure, if only because, among Christians, it could not do anything else; and the results were amazing. They extended gloriously into art, poetry, music, architecture. Here we are concerned only with the impact on ideas of the miraculous. Mary, it was commonly held, while remaining human even in her heavenly glory, could cause exceptions in the divine scheme more or less without limit. She could subvert not only nature but the spiritual order, the rule of divine law at the highest level. The power which was still God's alone could, through her, be virtually turned against him.

The logic of this view is worth examining. Mary's unique status was first put clearly into words by Germanus, who was Patriarch (Archbishop) of Constantinople in the eighth century. At that time the eastern Church, in the Byzantine Empire, was more intensely devoted to Mary than the western Church had yet become. Byzantine generals sought guidance from her before going into battle, and entrusted their forces to her care. Ships of the navy carried her image. For liturgical use a poet named Romanos had composed a long hymn in her honour, called the *Akathistos* (meaning 'not sitting', because everybody was expected to rise for it, like a national anthem). This hailed her as the source of all Christian truth, as the strength of martyrs, as the conqueror of demons, as the opener of paradise. In 626, when Constantinople beat off a barbarian siege, more verses were added to the hymn making it a song of thanksgiving. In 717 another siege was repelled, and Mary's influence in heaven was claimed more explicitly as the reason. The Patriarch Germanus held a festival in her honour, and preached a sermon making even loftier claims.

In effect he spoke of her as Co-Saviour with Christ. 'No one, Lady all-holy, is saved except through you.' Also he introduced two crucial ideas. Though not generally accepted at once, they grew more and more popular as the Middle Ages advanced, in the western Church as well as the eastern.

The first of his innovations was the setting up of Mary as an autonomous power, and, to most Christians, a more attractive one than God. He argued that God stood for Justice pure and simple, and since most of us are sinners, most of us are probably doomed to hell . . . that is, strictly according to the divine rules. But the rules need not worry us too much, because God's Mother, the Queen of Heaven, stands for Mercy and is willing to get them set aside. She can, and does, oppose God on man's behalf. Again Germanus addresses her: 'You turn away the just threat and the sentence of damnation, because you love the Christians . . . therefore the Christian people trustfully turn to you, refuge of sinners.'

To this we might object that however kind and merciful Mary may be, God has the last word. She may intercede for a sinner, but how does Germanus make out that she can actually quash the sentence on him? Moreover (to look at it from our present angle), since God is the only author of miracles, she cannot alter the course of nature for the sinner's benefit unless God agrees. She can only ask him. Germanus, however, has more to say. His other innovation is the astounding doctrine that Mary can give God orders. Christ obeyed her on earth. Therefore, as Second Person of the Trinity, he still obeys her in heaven. 'You, having maternal power with God, can obtain abundant forgiveness even for the greatest sinners. For he can never fail to hear you, because God obeys you through and in all things, as his true Mother.'

Two Gospel texts can be quoted in support of this notion. One, doubtless in Germanus's mind when he composed his sermon, is *Luke* 2:51. 'He went down with them' – that is, Mary and Joseph – 'and came to Nazareth, and was obedient to them; and his mother kept all these things in her heart.' This, however, refers only to Jesus's boyhood, not to the time of his adult ministry. The other text was pointed out three centuries before Germanus, and recurs after him as a mainstay for the theory of special Marian miracles. In *John* 2:1–11 we have the story of the wedding at Cana, where Christ performs his first 'sign'. Modern scholars have remarked that this changing of water into wine is a strange way for

83

Christ to declare himself. The miracle, with its huge surplus which the guests could not possibly have drunk, is like a public stunt or conjuring trick out of key with his later works of compassion and healing. However that may be, a detail which has often been seized upon is that Christ seems reluctant to perform it at all. It is his mother who says to him, 'They have no wine,' plainly urging him to do something. He replies brusquely, telling her that his time has not yet come. Refusing to take 'no' for an answer, she pushes him into action. Hence it may be inferred, and has been, that the Mother of God can actually command him to work a miracle.

Once proposed, such a privilege for Mary seemed to break God's monopoly. He might still be always involved, but when his Mother took an interest he became an executive for her rather than a sovereign in his own right. The novelty was never plainly admitted to be a novelty. Theologians who accepted it – and more and more did throughout Christendom, with ebullient popular support – managed to hold orthodoxy together by an ingenious formula. All miracles, they said, are indeed worked by God. His alone is the supreme power. Technically Mary is like the saints in general: she can only put requests to him. But she is different from all others because he never refuses what she asks. Therefore, for practical purposes, he obeys her even to the extent of suspending his own laws when she wants him to.

A modern theologian might try to soft-pedal this. He might say: 'Well, yes, but all it means is that the Virgin is supremely holy and completely at one with God. He never denies her, but that is only because she knows his will, and knows better than to make any request he would refuse.' That, however, is not how she was regarded by the popular Catholicism of the Middle Ages. In those days she had a will of her own and could make it felt. Since, through her devoted Son, she could obtain any favour she desired, she was omnipotent. Yet even so she was not divine herself, and that limitation gave her strength. Standing for Mercy against divine Justice, she was the champion of erring mankind. Although she had never sinned herself, she did still belong to our sinful species, and could arrange exceptions on its behalf all the more understandingly.

In western Europe the rise of Mary was gradual. At first her cult was almost confined to Italy. There are a few early traces of it in England. The first church at Glastonbury was dedicated to her, and a sixth-century cleric refers to someone swearing an oath at her shrine, probably in the church in question. Arthur is said to have carried her image into battle. But here and elsewhere, while Marian miracle-stories were coming into vogue as early as the tenth century, the tide did not flow strongly and decisively till the twelfth; and the theory that Mary can arrange anything, because God never says 'no' to her requests, appears among western writers about that time.

Two monks of the Benedictine Order propose it. Guibert of Nogent argues that God's own law binds him to carry out her wishes, because of his commandment – one of the Ten – to honour your father and mother. 'As a good son in this world so respects his mother's authority that she commands rather than asks, so he [Christ], who undoubtedly was once subject to her, cannot, I am sure, refuse her anything.' The other Benedictine, Geoffrey of Vendôme, cites both the Cana miracle and the Theophilus legend, and makes the slightly odd statement that although God is almighty he has never been able to refuse anything to his mother.

The great medieval upsurge of Marian worship did not favour such extreme notions from the beginning. They were some time coming into their own. In her splendid new cathedrals – Chartres, Reims, Amiens, Rouen, Bayeux, Paris – Mary reigned as Queen of Heaven, but without precise demarcation of her status. Dynastic chances, however, gave her celestial majesty a fresh aspect. In the later twelfth century one of the dominating figures of Europe was a Queen-Mother, Eleanor of Aquitaine. Towards the middle of the thirteenth a second Queen-Mother, Blanche of Castile, was a potent presence behind the sainted Louis IX. It was thus made easy for Mary to become Queen-*Mother* of Heaven, with Christ as her dutiful Son like Louis. The Trinity became subject to her persuasion in a way ordinary layfolk could grasp.

Meanwhile Christians had begun feeling a need for such a protectress, somewhat as those of the Roman Empire had when the Virgin was first enthroned. While the thirteenth century was an age of achievement, it was also an age of mounting disquiet. One traumatic disaster was the failure of the Crusades. Faith and zeal, in a series of religious wars, had at first won victories and given Christians a sense of divine blessing. But the converse was that when the infidels counter-attacked, regaining most of the lost ground, the blessing seemed to have been withdrawn. There was a new fear abroad, a sense of having somehow gone wrong, and come under God's censure. His love for his people was acknowledged in the abstract, but to many it was not evident. A similar sense of his remoteness was often keenly felt at the individual level. The Church's movement towards a rigid, legalistic system of doctrine made it look harder and harder to placate him, to win concessions from him, or to escape final doom. So the brightest hope lay in the Blessed Virgin, who was closer to erring mortals, sympathised with their weaknesses, was merciful where God was just, and could stand up to him in defence of those who loved her. Under the pressure of that need, the ideas of Germanus and the French monks were taken up and developed.

A scattered folklore of 'Miracles of Our Lady' already existed. In the thirteenth century, written collections were made, and the special character of these miracles became more apparent. The notion of Mary's power over God was entrenching itself in popular legend. One story tells how she literally went to visit her Son in heaven to ask a favour for somebody who had prayed to her ... as Queen-Mother Blanche might have gone to put in a word with King Louis for a dependant. Another tells how a group of devils complained about her. With God (the devils said) they knew where they were. They could rely on his justice, and if a soul was damned, he would hand it over to them. But Mary insisted on meddling, and cheating them of their prey. You never could tell when she would take it into her head to intercede for a sinner; and God (the devils further protested) 'loves and trusts her so much that he will never refuse or contradict her, whatever she does, whatever she says'.

This notion of beating the system is a recurring feature of her miracles. They carry on from Theophilus. Mary not only arranges exceptions in the way things happen, she arranges exceptions which come close to making God go against his own moral absolutes. Being able to get her way, she is superior to all the rules. She treats every case as a special case, and is apt to be partial to the very sinners whom God rejects, if they have the solitary virtue of loving her.

Quite often they have hardly anything else to commend them. Some medieval story-tellers enjoy blackening the characters she befriends, because it shows that the rest of us have no cause to despair. One legend concerns a robber who prays to her before going out thieving. He is caught, sentenced to death, and hanged. However, he does not fall to the length of the rope. After he has been suspended in mid-air for some time, unharmed, the hangman confesses a miracle and the thief is let off. In another legend a nun walks out of her convent and falls into sin. Her only link with the old life is that she never ceases to pray to Mary. At last, remorseful, she goes back to the convent expecting a harsh reception. But Mary has taken her place during her absence, looking exactly like her, and she has not been missed.

Our Lady smooths the way for the incompetent as well as the sinful. 'A certain half-witted priest,' as one story-teller puts it, was unequal to saying any Mass but the one which belonged to a Marian feast day in the calendar. So he went on repeating this Mass daily, till his bishop heard and suspended him. The priest prayed to Mary, and she appeared, saying: 'Go to the bishop and tell him from me to restore your office to you.' The priest protested that such a message would not be believed. She replied. 'I will prepare the way for you with a sign. When the bishop is mending his hair shirt I will hold one side to help him. Mention this to him, and he will know that we must have talked together.' The priest went to the bishop and spoke of Mary helping him with his mending. The bishop realised that their conversation must have taken place as reported. He allowed the priest to return to his church and go on as before, uncanonically saying the same Mass every day.

It is implied in these tales that Our Lady should be treated with great respect and even with flattery, and that the results of doing so can be spectacular, while the results of not doing so can be crushing. A Parisian cleric, we are told, greatly desired to see her. An angel came with the message that she would show herself to him, but the glory of her beauty would blind him. When she appeared, he covered one eye and saved it, but lost the sight of the other. Afterwards he had regrets, and said he would sacrifice the remaining eye to see her again. She returned to him, and, to reward his love, not only spared his second eye but restored the sight of the one he had lost. A story with a different emphasis tells of a man who was being pursued by three knights intent on killing him. He fled for sanctuary into a church dedicated to Mary. In this case, despite his trust in her, no miraculous rescue happened; the knights did kill him. But because of their disrespect for her church, she afflicted them with a raging fever. Full of contrition, they prayed to her for forgiveness, and she had mercy and the fever passed ... 'yet complete health was not restored to them.'

Obviously it is not likely that such things ever happened quite as described. They cannot be disproved, of course, and if we want to rationalise them we sometimes can. The illiterate priest may have tricked his bishop with the aid of a woman impersonating the Virgin. The knights' fever may have been a psychosomatic effect of guilt. However, that is not really the point. These legends of Our Lady are religious fairy-tales expressing an attitude, and the attitude matters more than the details.

Nor is it restricted to popular, wish-fulfilling fantasy. During the Middle Ages, authors of repute in the Church take this body of lore seriously and build up ideas on it. That is not to say that all of them do, or that extreme and credulous Marian notions are set up as official doctrine. Among theologians of the first rank, even those with a powerful Marian devotion, such as St Bernard, are firm about how far they will go. Followed magnificently by poets such as Dante and Petrarch, they salute Our Lady as a resplendent being, most glorious of creatures, supreme intercessor among the saints. But they never assign her a status in the cosmos which modifies the Christian conception of it. Others, however, do, and with an effect on the broad mass of believers out of proportion to the intrinsic value of their thought.

Thus Richard of St Laurent, a Rouen priest writing in the 1240s, says that the Christian scheme of things has actually altered because of Mary. It has become easier-going. 'Mary has so softened the Lord, and still continues to do so by her merits and prayers, that he now patiently tolerates even great sins, whereas before he mercilessly avenged even quite small ones.' Does this mean that she has interfered so much in the cosmic workings that her faithful worshippers can get away with anything, and Marian devotion is a licence to sin? That would be unfair. In the miracle-stories, where she helps 'her' sinners, she is theoretically giving them another chance, enabling them to repent and make their peace with God. However, this aspect is not always as clear as it might be. The sinner is very much 'hers', almost like a feudal dependant to whom she accepts an obligation. As a result the impression may well be that the sinner can eat his cake and have it, as Theophilus does, because, in the end, she will do something extraordinary to save him.

We may say: 'Well, at least there must have been limits making it risky. If the sinner died suddenly and went to hell, Mary could do nothing for him.' Yet in the popular medieval scheme, even this was by no means certain. Richard of St Laurent, echoing several of the miracle-stories, asserts that she has brought people back to life when their souls were already in the kingdom of Satan, so that they could do penance and get the verdict reversed.

No wonder the devils grumbled. Not only did she break the rules, she broke them in unpredictable ways that destroyed all certainty. The miracles of the Gospels, however starkly they defied common experience, had a logic about them. They were acts of God in the person of Christ, they could be explained as parts of a divine plan. Mary's were capricious. As a wonder-worker she stood not only for the irregular but for the all-too-human.

Indeed, she sometimes behaved in a human manner herself. In one legend a young man prays to her to make a girl look on him with favour, a change of heart which is, humanly speaking, impossible. Mary appears to him and says she is prepared to do something about it, but he must first decide which is more beautiful, the beloved or herself. If he chooses the beloved she will still comply with his wishes, but he may be in for trouble later. Other stories go further, suggesting that Mary's humanity is subject to the same lowly pressures as our own, even to a sort of blackmail. Thus, a widow's soldier son is captured by the enemy. The widow prays before a Madonna for his release. Nothing happens. So she removes the Child from the statue's embrace and holds it to ransom. Soon her son appears on the doorstep. It need not be supposed that the Virgin's arm has really been twisted by the kidnapping of a piece of wood from one of her countless images. She is gently amused at the mother's naïve conduct, and allows it to seem that the trick has worked ... but this means, in effect, that the trick *has* worked.

Faith in Mary's closeness and kindness could be exploited, and it was. Thus a particular local Madonna might become famous for granting prayers, to the profit of the clergy. Strictly speaking its reputation implied that Mary, for reasons of her own, chose to have a special care for people who knelt before that image. It gave them, so to speak, a hot line to her. However, the belief could easily slip into an idolatrous or magical trust in the actual object. The primitive-looking Black Madonnas acquired a special renown for wonder-working, perhaps because of their sheer strangeness. One of the best-known was at Montserrat in Catalonia (it is still there). Another, at Chartres, frightened the formidable Edward III. Another, at Dijon, was credited with routing a Swiss army. In the later Middle Ages the phenomenon became tragi-comic. Churches boasted of having Virgins that not only performed miracles – chiefly miraculous cures – but showed their approval of worshippers on the spot, by nodding or winking. Miracles of a kind were almost being performed to order. The Reformation swept away a great deal of this, and, in some cases, exposed deliberate fraud behind it. One of the English Madonnas was revealed to be operated like a ventriloquist's dummy by 'certain engines of rotten old sticks'.

Yet in all the fantasies and excesses of Mariolatry, a genuine idea was struggling to express itself. One could put it like this. Though the source of miracles is Beyond, not in ourselves, a human being might reach a level of attunement where the barrier would become unreal. God (whatever meaning we attach to the word) retains the sole power to work exceptions in nature. But the hypothetical person could be in such close rapport with him that an exception willed by that person would always happen.

In medieval Christendom such a rapport could only be conceived in terms of holiness, and there was only one person who could be allowed to possess it to that extent, Mary, Mother of God. Even then it was supposed to be confined to her post-earthly, glorified state. Yet we find Marian thoughts getting out of hand in that respect too. The idea of the incomparably superior human being, or the human being in total favour with God, encroaches on the story of Mary's career on earth, causing her to be pictured as entirely extraordinary even in her humble beginnings at Nazareth.

Such notions are by no means confined to spiritual matters. Some of her medieval adorers claim that was astoundingly beautiful, like Rider Haggard's 'She'. One of these is Richard of St Laurent, the same who says she can pull the damned out of hell. Forty pages of his book are taken up with her physical loveliness, which is given all sorts of symbolic meanings, and he suggests meditating on parts of her body as a spiritual exercise. A Greek cleric named Isidore Glabas makes this beauty frankly unearthly. As the chief of created beings, he argues, Mary might properly have been made first, but God did not place her in his world at the beginning because it could not have endured so much glory in its midst.

Other enthusiasts – quite a number in fact – credit her with knowledge and talents miraculous in themselves. Guibert of Nogent reasons that since she bore the omniscient God, she must have been omniscient too, though her humility held the gift in check. An anonymous writer, at about the same time as Richard of St Laurent, declares that 'the most blessed Virgin does not cede place to any of the famous in any matter whatsoever'. She had a perfect knowledge of the Trinity. She could see angels and devils. She understood scripture through and through. She foresaw her own future. She was the best mathematician, geographer and astronomer who ever lived. She was even expert in canon law, though the Church which drew it up did not yet exist.

In the fifteenth century a Franciscan friar, Bernardine of Busti, goes further still. When Mary was born, he assures us, she did not cry as babies do, but sang with the angels. At three years old she was mentally like a woman of thirty. She was fully informed in physics, metaphysics, logic, rhetoric, and indeed all subjects. The proof is simply that whatever knowledge God gave to anyone else, he must have given to Mary in a higher degree, so that she surpassed the human race in all subjects without having to learn them. Another Franciscan, Bernardine of Siena, says that Mary was sentient in the womb, and that 'even if she had not been the Mother of God, she would nevertheless have been the mistress of the world'.

Medieval fancies of this kind still restricted her powers of miracle-working on her own initiative to her glorified state in heaven after death. At last, however, even that restriction ceased to be maintained. Maria d'Agreda, the bilocating Spanish nun, wrote a 'life' of the Virgin based on private revelations, in which she asserted that as soon as Mary consented to bear God's Son he invested her with all knowledge and power, including the power to work any miracle she wished. So her omnipotence began on earth, at the age of fifteen or thereabouts. Though the Gospels do not record it, a series of miracles of her own formed a quiet accompaniment to Christ's.

What these Marian zealots were trying to do (though they would never have admitted it) was to square a theological circle. Starting with the Christian pattern as laid down, they were trying to fit a pre-Christian conception into it. Their enhanced Virgin was a resurgent figure out of a Goddess-oriented past, an age of numen and wisdom vested in the Female, of mysterious contact between the realms. She did not possess the metaphysical divinity of the Christian God. She did possess – or at any rate, recall – an older, less sharply outlined divinity. While the formula of 'God doing whatever Mary asks' held everything together after a fashion, the result was hardly biblical Christianity.

Mary-worship declined during the eighteenth century even in Catholic countries. It was revived, however, largely by St Alphonsus Liguori, an Italian priest of great learning, holiness and credulity. Marian devotion in modern times has owed a vast debt, psychologically at least, to his teachings.

St Alphonsus wrote a hymn to the Virgin which, despite ecumenical re-thinking, is still sung at Catholic gatherings. It begins 'O Mother blest', and includes this verse:

> Most powerful Mother, all men know
> Thy Son denies thee naught;
> Thou askest, wishest it and lo!
> His power thy will hath wrought.

Here is the medieval belief carrying on full-blown. However, Alphonsus's most solid work on this topic is a book entitled *The Glories of Mary*, published in 1750. Its basic thought is that 'God wants all graces to come to us by the hand of Mary'. God in principle offers heaven to mankind, but all arrangements go through her, and indeed she makes numerous decisions herself to which he merely gives a royal assent. 'Each of her prayers is, as it were, an established law for our Lord.' These prayers of hers are necessary for our salvation – not merely helpful, but necessary, though of course people are saved without knowing that she has prayed for them. The intercession of the saints is contingent on hers, to an extent that makes them seem hardly worth courting. Their prayers for us are channelled through her. Furthermore, if her concurrence is not seen to be forthcoming, they know better than to try. When Mary refrains from interceding for someone herself, none of the saints will venture to press the matter. When she does intercede, they add their voices to hers.

94

A mundane analogy that comes to mind is that of the 'assistant' to some tycoon whom few subordinates meet face to face. In theory, the assistant has no executive powers. In practice, the outer office may control almost everything. As a Christian, Alphonsus cannot very well say that his Tycoon is completely inaccessible without active wooing of the Assistant, but he comes close to it. He tells how a Franciscan saw a vision of two ladders. One was red with Christ at the top, the other was white with Mary at the top. A few persistent souls managed to climb the red ladder, but many more went up the white one, and Mary stretched out her hand and drew them into paradise. Elsewhere St Alphonsus re-states the idea of a virtually independent Virgin, opposing her own Mercy to divine Justice, restraining God's arm and holding back the sword. Sometimes, it appears, he is grateful to her for checking him in his wrath against sinners and allowing a cooling-off period. 'Mary ... knows so well how, by tender and soothing prayers, to appease the divine justice, that God himself blesses her for it and, as it were, thanks her for having prevented him from abandoning and chastising them as they deserved.'

Ostensibly, still, the purpose of her acts of mercy is not to give the sinner licence to sin but to give him a further chance to repent, which he is all the more likely to do after she has shown him such kindness. But Alphonsus carries his ideas to a point where they shift the balance of Christianity. He revives the medieval popular notions and takes them further. In his many stories of Mary's miracles, and other gracious deeds, the most casual nod in her direction seems enough to outweigh all sins and even give the sinner an advantage over the virtuous. A reader wonders why anybody should bother to be good.

One story tells how a man neglected all morality and religious duty for fifty-five years, except that he used to salute images of the Virgin and beg her not to let him die in his sins. When he was fighting an enemy his sword

95

broke. He prayed to her to save him, and she whisked him off through the air to a place of safety. Having made his overdue confession he died at peace. In another story, one of the most significant, Alphonsus tells of a woman whose husband was having an affair. She prayed before an image of Mary for justice against her rival. The rival, however, was in the habit of saying Hail Marys before the same image. Mary appeared to the wife in a dream and reproved her for offering prayers for justice: she did not regard justice as her concern, and preferred the Hail Marys of the guilty party. Next day the wife met the mistress, accused her of witchcraft, and told her about the dream. Impressed by the efficacy of the Hail Marys, the mistress offered her apologies and put an end to the affair.

What exactly is the moral of this second tale? Of course there is the suggestion of better behaviour at the end, but the mistress has got away with it by simply reciting a set prayer from time to time, and no retribution comes to her. Some of the stories have no real ethical content at all. Thus we are told of a man who was about to be imprisoned for debt. There is no indication whether this was because of bad luck, bad judgment, or dishonesty. He prayed to Mary, she inspired his creditors to let him off what he owed them . . . and that is the whole story.

The Virgin works miracles for her friends even when all seems lost. Alphonsus asks us to believe in a robber whose enemies cut his head off when he was in a state of sin, and whom Mary still rescued from divine justice, because, pleased at some fasting he had done in her honour, she kept his severed head alive in a ditch and a priest heard its confession. Apparently she is known to save people against their will, with no conscious good intention whatever – as in the case of a man who said a Hail Mary morning and evening, and, when about to renew his acquaintance with a former mistress, was driven back from her door 'by an invisible power' and propelled the whole length of the street. The *reductio ad absurdum* of Alphonsus's anecdotes is one about a magpie which was taught to say 'Ave Maria'. One day the bird was being chased by a hawk. At the last gasp it happened to croak 'Ave Maria', whereupon the hawk dropped out of the air, dead.

In many such tales the shift away from a truly God-centred order is becoming more palpable, though Alphonsus would have been shocked at anyone thinking so. Law, integrity, even love in its more stalwart forms, tend to be replaced by a childish clinging to someone other than God. A high proportion of the characters burst into tears at crucial moments. The general feeling is that humanity is too weak, too irresponsible, for a direct and mature relationship with its Maker. Its best hope lies in keeping on the right side (however perfunctorily) of a being who is all-powerful, but still human herself – that is the point. Through the 'Mother blest' who is its supreme representative, it can find a short cut to salvation which, in effect, dispenses with God. He is still there as the goal of the human pilgrimage, but the rules he has laid down for this are by-passed. As for the miracles, he is still technically behind them, but in stories such as the magpie anecdote, an older magical world is reinstated.

The Glories of Mary was a popular book, and the ardour it expressed gained ground slowly among Catholics till it affected policy at the summit. From 1854, when Pope Pius IX defined Mary's Immaculate Conception, to 1950, when Pius XII defined her Assumption, a new wave of Marian devotion rose in the Church. Less has been heard on the topic since John XXIII, but the doctrines and speculations which were being aired before his accession have never been condemned. Some of the extremer vagaries were, indeed, soft-pedalled. The moral atmosphere improved – there was less of the implication that bad characters could get away with anything by saying a regular Hail Mary – and the opposition of Mary's mercy to God's justice was dropped. Yet in the judgment of some historians of the cult, its strange backhanded humanism increased rather than lessened. The Virgin tended to grow so great and wonderful that her Son himself no longer had anything distinctive about him, except his abstract divinity. The motif of the supremely exalted human being – the human being exalted to the point of total rapport with the divine Beyond – reappeared in new forms.

Theologians no longer tried to make out that Mary was a superwoman in knowledge and talents. But they heaped her with other qualities which, in their scale of values, counted for more. Thus in the pontificate of Pius XII, Father Gabriele Roschini proposed four principles to govern thinking about her. These were:

1. Singularity. Mary is unique and has privileges no other creature possesses, or can possess.

2. Appropriateness. Whatever perfections we can think of which would be suitable to her, and not repugnant to the general Catholic view of things, we must assume she actually has. (This seems to apply to her earthly life as well as her state in glory. Roschini resurrects the medieval idea that she must have been physically beautiful.)

3. Eminence. Not only is she higher than all the saints, she surpasses them all in every respect. Therefore, whatever special distinction any saint has, Mary has it too and more so.

4. Analogy to Christ. Whatever special qualities her Son had as a human being, she shared.

In Roschini's view Mary was above everything whatever except God himself. Her greatness 'bordered on the infinite'. Other Catholics argued that she completed the Trinity by making it fruitful; or that as the scheme of redemption would have been imperfect without both sexes taking part, she supplied the female aspect of human nature. On this ground and others she came to be widely regarded as Co-Redemptress with Christ.

Once again, feminists may urge that this exaltation was bogus, conserving male status by setting up a false and artificial female ideal; but once again, the priestly theorising was not what the Marian resurgence was really about. In popular devotion Mary was never an ideal anyway. She was living humanity, in an apotheosised female aspect, wielding supernatural power.

Her reality to the faithful is shown by the series of apparitions which began in 1830. To Catholics of the past century and a half, Christ has appeared rarely but the Virgin often. Moreover she has appeared alone, or, if not alone, as the unrivalled principal figure in whatever is seen. She is a person in her own right. The first of her modern manifestations took place in 1830 at a convent in Paris. The seer was a twenty-four-year-old nun, Catherine Labouré. In 1846 Mary was seen by two children at La Salette. In 1858 she appeared at Lourdes, in 1871 at Pontmain, in 1917 at Fatima in Portugal, in 1932 at Beauraing in Belgium, and in 1933 at Banneux, also in Belgium. Beauraing was the first in a stream of alleged appearances running to about thirty, though in every other instance, except Banneux, ecclesiastical authorities received them coolly.

Apart from Catherine Labouré at the beginning of the series, most of the seers have been very young. With one or two outstanding exceptions Mary's reported speeches and actions have not sounded at all likely. The irreducible point of interest is that modern Catholic fantasy, or whatever it is, should have taken such a form, should have focused on the human-being-in-total-rapport-with-the-divine rather than on divinity itself. We might leave the topic there, if it were not for a fact of a more specific nature. In two major cases the Virgin's advent has been followed by miracles. These are not like the legendary ones of the Middle Ages. They have occurred in public view, and sometimes under what is claimed to be scientific scrutiny.

5

The Spring and the Sun

Lourdes is a French town in the approaches of the Pyrenees, ten miles from Tarbes. It nestles among moderate-sized mountains in a setting which is beautiful without being overpowering. A small swift river, the Gave, runs through it. At the middle of the nineteenth century the town lay wholly on one side of the river and was much smaller, with about four thousand inhabitants. The only importance it had ever possessed was as a military strong point, a fact attested by its castle.

Today the permanent population is nearly twenty thousand. The town spreads widely on both sides of the Gave, and has a capacity for visitors which would be hard to match in any other place the same size. Beside the water is a long, enclosed, lovingly tended rectangle of lawn and trees, and at the end of this is a tall grey basilica which is not merely a church but three churches, one above another, entered by a complication of stairs and ramps. To the right as you approach is a broad paved promenade. If you go along it, past the base of the triple church, you come to the scene of the events that caused this transformation.

Bernadette Soubirous was born in 1844 near the castle, the first child of a miller. The family were practising Catholics but in no way devout. Her father's poor management and (allegedly) drinking led to the loss of the mill, and a poverty-stricken existence in a disused prison. Damp and malnutrition affected Bernadette's health. At fourteen she was undersized and asthmatic. However, she was able to work in the open, looking after sheep.

On February 11th, 1858, a Thursday, she went out with a younger sister and a friend to gather firewood.

They walked through what was then open country to a point where a canal branched off from the River Gave. On the opposite side of the canal was a patch of bare rock-face, with a natural grotto in it called Massabielle. This consisted (and still does) of a large recess, hardly deep enough to be called a cave, with niches and clefts in the rock above it. Although the place was within walking distance of her home, Bernadette had never been there before, and it had no special associations for her. The two other children saw some driftwood lying on the far bank near the grotto, and waded over the shallow canal. Bernadette was reluctant to follow because the water was cold, but she finally took off her shoes and stockings and was about to begin wading, when there was an interruption. The following is an abridgement of her own account of it.

I heard the sound of wind, as in a storm. I turned towards the meadow and saw that the trees were not moving at all. . . . I was putting one foot into the water when I heard the same sound in front of me. I looked up and saw a cluster of branches and brambles underneath the highest opening of the grotto tossing and swinging to and fro, although nothing else stirred.

Behind these branches and inside the opening, I saw at that moment a girl in white, no bigger than myself, who greeted me with a slight bow of her head. At the same time she stretched out her arms slightly away from her body, opening her hands as in a picture or statue of Our Lady. Over her right arm hung a rosary. I was afraid and drew back. . .

Looking up I saw the girl smiling at me most graciously and seeming to invite me to come nearer. But I was still afraid. It was not a fear such as I have felt at other times, however, for I would have stayed there for ever looking at her. . . .

Then I thought of saying my prayers. I put my hand in my pocket and took out the rosary I always have with me. . . . I said my rosary. The girl passed the beads through her fingers but she did not move her lips. . . .

She was wearing a white dress right down to her feet and only the tips of her toes were showing. The dress was gathered high at the neck from which there hung a white cord. A white veil covered her head and came down over her shoulders and arms almost to the bottom of her dress. On each foot I saw a yellow rose. The sash of the dress was blue and hung down below her knees. The chain of the rosary was yellow, the beads white and big, and widely spaced.

The girl was alive, very young and surrounded with light. When I had finished my rosary she bowed to me smilingly. She retired within the niche, and suddenly disappeared.

This is a touching narrative, and it shows to advantage beside those of some other purported seers. It calls, however, for several comments. We might wonder how Bernadette, who had neither unusual eyesight nor trained powers of observation, could make out so much detail from a fair distance off across the water. The fact is, even her own story does not actually imply that she did. She told it in this form – piecemeal, not consecutively – several days afterwards, when she had seen the figure again from a point much closer. Speaking to her confessor on the Saturday after the first appearance, she was far less precise, saying only that it was 'something white in the shape of a girl'. In her favour it should be stressed that she never asserted it to be the Virgin. Her own habitual term for it was 'Aqueró', meaning, in the local patois, 'this thing'. Another detail suggesting more than mere invention at work, or normal imagination for that matter, is the touch about the figure counting the rosary beads with Bernadette but not saying the prayers with her. Since most of the prayers are Hail Marys, it might be presumed that Mary would not address them to herself. Yet such a thought seems very sophisticated for a country child almost without schooling.

There is no real proof as to how long the vision lasted. It may be doubted whether Bernadette said the entire rosary, an exercise which takes at least twenty minutes. Her two companions, however, looking back across the water, had seen her kneeling motionless for a long enough time to be disturbing. When the apparition vanished she finally waded over to join them, and the wood-gathering was completed. Bernadette asked if they had seen anything (they had not) and then, hesitantly, told them the vision. Rumours spread. Her parents were annoyed and at first forbade her to return to the spot, but on Sunday they relented, not very happily. She went round by another route with a bottle of holy water, and scrambled down to the grotto from the hillside above. The figure appeared again, though several girls who had accompanied her saw nothing – not even, it seems, any disturbance of the wild rose bush under the niche. The holy water had no banishing effect. Bernadette knelt for some time in an ecstasy, weeping and smiling together.

In all there were eighteen of these appearances. On the third occasion the Lady spoke, in a 'very gentle voice', with grave courtesy. She addressed Bernadette as 'vous', not familiarly as 'tu', promising to make her happy in the next world but not in this. Despite hostility from the civic officialdom, more and more people came to witness Bernadette's ecstasies. One day a sceptical doctor took her pulse and tested her respiration, but found both to be normal. Back in the town the Commissioner of Police subjected her to a searching questioning without being able to shake her story. Though no onlookers ever saw the Lady, many testified to a transfiguring beauty that came over Bernadette – a plain child – during her ecstasies, and were persuaded that she was communicating with someone or something.

On February 25th the Lady told her to 'drink and wash at the spring', and indicated a spot on the ground where only a puddle could be seen. Bernadette scratched with her hand. A little water began to flow and, though muddy at first, gradually became clear and more plentiful. The Lady's next request was for the building of a chapel. Bernadette passed it on to the parish priest, the Abbé Peyramale. He was strongly opposed to the whole performance, and told her to find out the Lady's name. 'If she thinks she has any right to a chapel,' he added, 'ask her from me to prove it by making the rose bush at the grotto flower immediately.' The next day she conveyed the request, but the Lady only smiled.

This curious deadlock over the name lasted for sev-

103

eral weeks, and the apparitions seemed to have stopped. But the flow of visitors continued, and the Soubirous parents were accused of making money out of their daughter's visions, though the charge was disproved. On March 25th Bernadette went to the grotto, and a crowd of onlookers saw her go into ecstasy once more. This time the Lady moved downward from her niche in the rock and hovered in the arch of the grotto itself, much nearer. Bernadette asked her name, three times, and at the third request there was at last a reply: 'I am the Immaculate Conception' (in the patois, *Immaculada Concepciou*).

When Bernadette told the priest, he was shaken. The dogma of the Immaculate Conception asserts that Mary, alone among human beings, was not only sinless but exempted even from the original sin which, supposedly, we all have from the first instant of life. Hence, the words 'Immaculate Conception' would point to the Blessed Virgin and no one else. This doctrine, widely held in the Catholic Church for centuries, had been defined by the Pope four years before the visions. But the cumbersome phrase would have been a curious thing for an unlettered child to hit on as a sort of code designation. Bernadette in fact had no conscious memory of it at all, and repeated it to the priest parrot-wise.

The Bishop of Tarbes, in whose diocese Lourdes was, felt obliged to consider the case more seriously. He was under great pressure from enthusiasts, and silence was no longer enough. The civic authorities tried to fence off the grotto, so as to gain at least a breathing-space, but their barriers were broken down. A first physical miracle or quasi-miracle occurred there on April 7th. Bernadette was again in ecstasy, and a candle she was holding slipped down through her fingers so that the flame was visibly burning her hand. She showed no sign of feeling it, and the sceptical doctor, who was present again, found her hand to be unmarked. A little later a farmer brought his five-year-old paralytic son to the grotto, and plunged him into the water now flowing copiously from the spring Bernadette had opened. Almost at once he stood up and walked.

The Lady made her last appearance on July 16th. Bernadette was not aware of any special leave-taking, but apparently understood that this was the end, though she continued afterwards to revisit the grotto from time to time. She went on living in Lourdes till her entry into a convent in 1866. A commission which the Bishop of Tarbes had set up had already reached its conclusion.

> We judge that Mary, the Immaculate Mother of God, did really appear to Bernadette Soubirous on February 11th 1858 and on certain subsequent days – to the number of eighteen times in all – in the grotto of Massabielle, near the town of Lourdes; that this Apparition bears every mark of truth and that the faithful are justified in believing it as certain.

Even in an age when Rome was far more authoritative than it is now, this verdict was permissive rather than mandatory. A commission appointed by one French bishop was not the Church. Catholics have never been obliged to agree with it, or to place any supernatural construction on the sequel. What the Bishop chiefly did was to put an end to attempts at suppression, and allow a cult to unfold in a benign atmosphere. Its best known feature had been foreshadowed while the apparitions were still going on. Not automatically, not even frequently, but persistently in the face of ridicule, sick people who were dipped in the water underwent amazing recoveries.

Lourdes rose quickly in esteem as a place of pilgrimage. The process was by no means smooth. Unedifying disputes broke out between rival branches of the clergy, over the building of new churches and the right to provide facilities for the pilgrims. Growth, however, went on unchecked, and as reports spread about the springwater effecting cures, more and more stress was laid on that aspect. Presently a bath-house was built, and whole parties of sick pilgrims began to arrive in special trains.

Societies of lay volunteers were formed, who helped in conducting the sick to Lourdes and looking after them during their stay. Further building, and improvements in organisation, have continued into modern times.

Cures undoubtedly happen at Lourdes, and some have been medically surprising, to say the least. But have any been miracles? The first step towards an answer is to clear away irrelevancies.

To begin with, there is no question of Lourdes being some kind of spa. The water from the spring is in no way special. It was analysed at an early stage of the excitement, and found to be plain mountain water typical of the Pyrenees. More recent analysis has confirmed this finding. Its small mineral content does not make it 'spa' water, nor has it any abnormal ingredients, such as mould, which might give it curative powers. The argument (which I have actually heard) that 'there can't be anything extraordinary about Lourdes, because analysis has shown that the water is just water', would be hard to beat for fatuity. The water *is* just water, and that is one of the reasons why Lourdes is extraordinary.

Such simple material causes can be dismissed. Where the difficulties begin is over the question of 'faith-healing'. This is a natural term to apply to the Lourdes cures, and it often is. However, it must be used with discrimination. It suggests a kind of healing which, if it could be shown to account for all the cases, would not confirm the miraculous but banish it. Healing of this type is commonly the work of a healer, such as an evangelist or a layer-on of hands. It is a therapeutic technique which sometimes works when the disorder is, broadly speaking, nervous rather than physical. The cure may be brilliant, as when a paralytic patient gets up and walks, but when this happens it is because an inhibition has been dispelled, not because the limbs have altered. An X-ray would show nothing.

Psychosomatic cures like this – faith-healing cures properly so called – can occur without the presence of a practitioner, and at Lourdes they doubtless have, in large numbers. Much can be put down to the effects of sheer atmosphere and mass suggestion. The actual sick are only the conspicuous minority in a swarm of pilgrims who vastly outnumber them. They are tens of thousands among millions. It is easy for these few to be uplifted in spirit and swept along by the many.

However (and this is the point which is far too seldom grasped), such cures are not claimed as miracles. The ecclesiastical authorities know as well as anyone that they happen in the course of nature, not through any special divine act. A Lourdes miracle is only officially declared – and even then, belief is not made binding upon the faithful – when such explanations have been ruled out, together with all others which medical science can propose. This policy is in keeping with principles we have already noted. Science can never positively prove a miracle, because, by definition, miracles are exceptions and outside science. On the other hand, when all its own explanations have failed, it has forfeited the right to deny. Belief or disbelief must then be on other grounds: whether the event has the right sort of character and meaning, what its sequels are, and so forth.

A doctor named Saint-Maclou set up the first regular Lourdes procedure in 1885. He and his successors maintained an office where pilgrims claiming to have been cured were examined. Attempts were made to check their medical history. It was all very slipshod, and often the medical history was no more than a brief opinion from a third-rate country GP, warped one way or the other by his own bias. Still, the cumulative effect of the cases these doctors studied inclined them to acknowledge a mystery, and they sometimes did so in writing, commenting on particular patients.

Émile Zola's novel *Lourdes* gives a readable picture of the state of affairs in 1892. It is not so much fiction as fictionalised documentary, by an acute, hostile, but compassionate journalist. When interviewed about it, Zola admitted that he had come across several indisputable cures. For him the problem was not of fact but of in-

107

terpretation. His judgment was that owing to medical ignorance, gaps in testimony, and other factors, the asserted miracles could be neither proved nor disproved. That being so, the rational course was to reject them. He did not believe in them himself. Many did, not actually against the facts, nor through deception or self-deception, but because of wishful thinking. Human need, human despair, would always tend to clutch at the affirmative option and detect the hand of the Blessed Virgin.

Zola presents this conclusion through a character in the story.

> Pierre had now begun to understand what was taking place at Lourdes. . . . Forces as yet but imperfectly studied, of which one was even ignorant, were certainly at work – auto-suggestion, long prepared disturbance of the nerves; inspiriting influence of the journey, the prayers and the hymns; and especially the healing breath, the unknown force which was evolved from the multitude, in the acute crisis of faith. Thus it seemed to him anything but intelligent to believe in trickery. The facts were both of a much more lofty and much more simple nature. There was no occasion for the Fathers of the Grotto to descend to falsehood; it was sufficient that they should help in creating confusion, that they should utilise the universal ignorance. It might even be admitted that everybody acted in good faith – the doctors void of genius who delivered the certificates, the consoled patients who believed themselves cured, and the impassioned witnesses who swore that they had beheld what they described. And from all this was evolved the obvious impossibility of proving whether there was miracle or not. And such being the case, did not the miracle naturally become a reality for the greater number, for all those who suffered and who had need of hope?

In other places, Zola rather spoils his impartial effect. For instance, when recalling how the whole business began, he has to reckon with the fact that the Bishop of Tarbes, a wise and enlightened prelate, authorised the cult when he might have stopped it. Zola cannot admit that such a man might have believed in the apparitions. So he resorts to speculation about the Bishop's state of mind under popular pressure ('How great must have been his anguish', etc.), and contends that he allowed pity to overrule reason, 'granting that bread of falsehood which poor humanity requires in order to be happy'. This seems to be pure fantasy, wishful thinking by the sceptic instead of the believer. Zola is also quoted as having said, not in the novel, 'If all the sick at Lourdes were cured simultaneously I would still not believe' – an amusing unconscious comment on the sceptic's posture of open-mindedness. Nevertheless, *Lourdes* remains a most interesting book, making points which are still valid. The account of Bernadette herself is strangely and unexpectedly moving, almost as if, here alone, a conviction of the supernatural very nearly forced its way through and had to be resisted.

For about sixty years the situation remained as Zola portrayed it, though the Medical Bureau grew somewhat more systematic and cautious. As a rule, its opinion as to whether a cure could be naturally explained was the final step in inquiry. From 1925 to 1938 it denied that possibility in eighty-five cases. When it had done so, belief in a miracle was a matter of choice, and the Church seldom made any pronouncement. Medical men of the highest eminence were impressed, the Nobel prizewinner Alexis Carrel, for instance. Others were not.

Shortly after the Second World War, with the renewal of mass pilgrimage, the procedure was tightened up and elaborated. A group of Catholic specialists went through the files and found much to criticise. Sick pilgrims were henceforth encouraged to bring certificates from their own doctors, giving a full appraisal, so that in the event of a cure the nature of the physical change could be defined. Under a new head, Dr François Leuret, the Medical Bureau was expanded and re-equipped. More important perhaps was the addition of two more hurdles which a reputed miracle had to clear, with an ecclesiastical statement at the end of the course. An International Medical Commission was set up, with headquarters in Paris. Henceforth, if the Medical

Bureau on the spot found a cure sufficiently hard to explain, it passed the patient's dossier to the new Commission. If the doctors assembled in Paris also judged it inexplicable, the dossier went to the archbishop of the diocese where the patient lived. He would then order a special inquiry into the background. Only if this revealed no new data to modif / the doctors' judgment, or raise queries of other kinds, could there be any question of admitting a miracle.

This procedure narrowed the field. Only about one-tenth of the cures studied at Lourdes got as far as the International Commission. Less than half that fraction got through to the archbishops. Even then the local inquiries were as likely as not to lead to a negative result. In the first decade of the new system, only eleven cases survived all three scrutinies, and were declared by Church authorities to be acceptable as miracles. The record for the following decade was much the same. Since 1965 it does not appear that the long-drawn procedure has been pushed through to the end so often, and final figures are not available to the same extent.

To count as a miracle, a cure must satisfy the conditions laid down by Pope Benedict XIV in his rules for canonisation (page 73). In practice the suddenness of change is the aspect likeliest to be reckoned important. The cases judged miraculous from 1946 to 1955 were critically dissected by Dr D.J. West in a study entitled *Eleven Lourdes Miracles.* The later ones have not been similarly treated in English.

The eleven are as follows. Women predominate, as they always have, but too much should not be made of this. More women than men go on pilgrimages.

Mlle Gabrielle Clauzel: spinal arthritis.
Mme Gestas: post-gastrectomy disturbances.
Mme Rose Martin: secondary cancer.
Francis Pascal: paralysis from meningitis.
Colonel Pellegrin: fistula.
Sister Marguerite: nephritis.

110

Mlle Thérèse Canin: peritoneal tuberculosis.
Mlle Louise Jamain: pulmonary tuberculosis.
Mlle Jeanne Fretel: peritoneal tuberculosis.
Fräulein Fulda: Addison's disease.
Mme Couteault: disseminated sclerosis.

Dr West's discussion of these cures raises technical issues beyond our present scope. He is careful to stress that opinions differ. Broadly speaking his conclusion is that they must differ, because the evidence is never precise enough, and is certainly not as precise as advocates of Lourdes like to maintain. None of the miracles are obvious ones, medically incredible at a glance, like a patient's growing a replacement for a lost limb. The sudden clearing-up of a cancer or a tubercular condition may be genuine, but it does not show. To make out a case for a miracle, there has to be a proof of complete abnormality which is by no means simple. While the eleven cures were all clearly remarkable, Dr West argues that three major obstacles stand in the way of proper assessment.

First, the case-histories are never quite adequate. Diagnosis may have been wrong, or there may have been unknown factors which inquiry never brought to light. Second, there is the old psychosomatic problem – how far a cure could have been due to a state of mind induced by Lourdes. None of the eleven cases suggest this, but scientists have learned to be wary of fixing limits to such phenomena. Third, there is the lack of experimental control. Patients recover suddenly and mysteriously at Lourdes, but patients recover suddenly and mysteriously at other places. We have no means of knowing whether the Lourdes patients would or would not have done so if they had stayed at home.

In the cures studied by Dr West, the miraculous explanation has never been exploded. Not one has been definitely traced to a natural cause, such as treatment suppressed in the Lourdes reports but unmasked by independent investigation. The remark of Bernard Shaw's

111

archbishop about 'knowing how it is done' certainly does not apply. However, the element of doubt is always present and sometimes serious. We must conclude that the miraculous claims of Lourdes have not been strictly proved one way or the other, even in the sense of its being quite certain whether scientists and doctors can or cannot explain every happening. Most of them (as is their habit) evade the issue. Among those who have faced it, names of distinction can be quoted on both sides. Zola's verdict is still tenable. Perhaps, though, a certain sorting-out has occurred. Most of the alleged miracles since 1858 can be passed over, but the few that survive are more impressive. Belief – a sober, discriminating belief – is more respectable than in Zola's time and less wishful. That remains true in spite of the gaps that may have been revealed in the evidence.

It must be added finally that to make everything depend on the handful of miracles is to get Lourdes out of perspective, even if they are all authentic. Lourdes is a place of bodily and spiritual healing – for uncounted thousands, not merely for a few special cases – which it is futile to dismiss. The Presence (I do not know what else to call it) is far greater than any aggregate of single events. With all the influx of the diseased, there has never been an epidemic. Dean Inge, an Anglican churchman and author of some note between the wars, once showed his Christian charity by describing Lourdes as a 'lucrative imposture'. Few who have honestly examined the facts would echo him today. Even the famous commercialism, with its attendant tawdriness, is far less garish than outsiders are apt to think.

G. K. Chesterton (whom the same Dean Inge, always the scholar and gentleman, called an 'obese mountebank') visited Lourdes in 1936. He had long shied away from such a visit because of what he had heard of the place. On seeing it at last, he put his impressions in a letter which still, despite many changes, has a truth observed with profundity and wit.

112

Lourdes is *not* spoilt: Our Lady came here to the very humblest, to a ragged child almost barefoot: and perhaps that is why there is a sense that she has left this rocky place in a naked purity like stone; as if there were health and not wealth to be got out of it. .... At Lourdes the framework is hard rock and Holy Poverty – all that Assisi ought to be. Of course there are shops that sell souvenirs: that is inevitabe: for we must all sympathise with those who buy if not with those who sell. But something has put the Fear of God into the shop-keepers: they do not tout or push or haggle or even, as a rule, appear. ...

Whoever organised the thing showed great restraint. The Grotto is not a 'blaze of gold and tinsel' as it is its duty to be for the sake of Baptist tourists from Tennessee. The Grotto is a grey forest of crutches and wooden legs hung up by ex-cripples who could only afford such things in honest wood. The rest is the lies of journalists (like me) and especially the lies of photographers. For nothing can lie like the camera. I had a notion that a colossal statue dominated the town, an Eiffel Tower lit up like a lighthouse. This was done by somebody tilting a camera in front of a small quiet statue in an enclosed space, a space as quiet and cut off as a Retreat. Forgive me for boring on in this way: but I am filled with a sort of surprise as well as indignation.

Fatima, the Church's other modern miraculous venue, is a different case. Its claim rests on a single startling event, which was reported in the newspapers of the day, but is hard to parallel outside even in legend. As there is nothing to compare it with, it presents a problem which has been generally recoiled from, even by thoughtful Catholics, who are aware of the difficulties. Yet it is doubtful whether any other miracle ever happened so publicly, so spectacularly, before such a large audience, or with such crushing effect (at the time) on the opposition.

Fatima is a village in the high country of central Portugal. Unlike Lourdes it has little scenic attraction. The landscape is stony, with small trees and rather sparse vegetation. It undulates gently without ever rising into high hills or sinking into deep valleys. No large town is near. In 1917 at the time of the visitation, the peasants lived hard-working frugal lives and were not conspicuously pious or fanciful. Today, thanks to the events of that year, Fatima has a massive basilica with a huge, bare court for assemblages of pilgrims. Shops and guesthouses are round about as at Lourdes, but the prevailing effect remains austere.

As with Lourdes, the first datum is a story of apparitions. There is no need here for a detailed account of them. Judgment on such things must be, to some extent, personal. Many who have considered these, however, feel that whereas the Lourdes narrative has an air of honesty even if it is honesty about delusions, the Fatima narrative is suspect.

The chief seer was Lucia dos Santos, a girl of ten. Two younger cousins, Francisco and Jacinta, partly shared her experiences. On May 13th, 1917, the three were tending sheep in the Cova da Iria, a valley or rather depression some distance from the village. They saw a flash of light followed by another, and then Lucia and Jacinta, but not the boy, saw 'a pretty little lady' standing in the air above a small tree. She said she came from heaven, and asked the children to visit the same place on the thirteenth of each month. On the sixth occasion she would tell them who she was.

As at Lourdes the story spread, and when the children kept their appointments, they trailed an increasing crowd of spectators. The Lady made various requests, the only one not a pious cliché being to say the rosary for peace. The First World War was still in progress with no end in sight, and Portugal had recently entered it. Lucia described her as wearing a white dress with gold borders, and a gold cord round the neck. Her head was covered with a white veil but her face was fully in view. In September she promised a miracle for October 13th. It is this miracle – which certainly happened in some sense, and ensured that Fatima would become a place of devotion and pilgrimage – that calls for scrutiny here. The context may mostly be set aside. Historically speaking, it is not much use doing anything else, because the story has been overlaid with second thoughts and

114

'interpretations', which have obscured the facts beyond accurate recovery.

Lucia's visions – so far as their nature can be established – sound like an imitation of Bernadette's. The presence of the two other children complicates matters further. Jacinta and Francisco both saw something, though it is not clear exactly what or when; Lucia seems to have done all the talking. Whatever the truth, the accompaniments and sequels have piled confusion on confusion. Portugal in 1917 was going through a phase of violent anti-clericalism in high places, and the Fatima events were embroiled in politics from the start. An atheist local administrator treated the children with senseless cruelty and made martyrs of them. Later, during the clerical reaction, Fatima became a prized asset of Salazar's dictatorship. In 1936–7 and 1941–2, Lucia, who had become a Carmelite nun, divulged further details which she had never mentioned before. The Lady was credited with a speech warning against Communism – 'Russia spreading her errors through the world'. If this had been reported during the visions, when Lenin's revolution lay in the future, it would have been an arresting prophecy. It was not. The alleged anti-Communist warning was only published when the Red Menace had become a prime Catholic concern.

Lucia also wrote out a further revelation which was to be kept secret till 1960. As the crucial year approached, it was whispered that the sealed paper foretold a Third World War. Several wealthy American Catholics are said to have transferred their money to Portugal, in the belief that it was the only country with a celestial guarantee against Communist conquest. 1960. however, came and went and Lucia's envelope remained as mysterious as before.

Soon afterwards the guessing began. According to rumour it had been opened, probably at the Vatican, but the words written on the paper inside were never given out because they were in conflict with the Church's current position, or even damaging in a more

115

profound sense. Some journalists favoured a theory that they foretold the return of all Christians to the Roman fold, an idea at odds with the new ecumenism and Rome's efforts to come to terms with Protestants. Later another journalist claimed that they foretold a great apostasy at the heart of the Catholic Church: the Antichrist himself would become Pope. After decades of Catholic insistence on the Fatima revelations as true, Rome could hardly have published that. But in spite of all such stories, the secret remained secret. With the failure of this and other specific prophesyings, the Fatima message was reduced to a vague call for 'penance, prayer, hope'.

The point of bearing these facts in mind, when examining the miracle which the Lady promised and delivered, is not that they give it a setting and a meaning but that they utterly fail to do so. It stands up in stark extraordinariness, with nothing else relevant or convincing, before or after, to make sense of it.

Though the weather was wet on October 13th, Lucia's announcement brought seventy thousand people to the spot. Thanks to the months of growing publicity the crowd included many besides the naïvely pious. A number of priests had come, aware that a fiasco would make their position even weaker, and anxious to know the worst at once. Atheists came hoping for the same disaster which the priests dreaded. Sceptical professors, a few doctors, and an eye specialist had also arrived, as well as a squad of journalists. Among the last was Avelino de Almeida, editor of *O Seculo*, the principal anti-clerical paper. That morning's issue carried an article he had written drawing attention to Fatima, so as to give the expected failure maximum impact.

Lucia waited. Her heavenly friend appeared, said she was 'the Lady of the Rosary' (another phrase like 'the Immaculate Conception' which uniquely designates Mary), and, according to the child, also said that the war was ending that day – an error which, if it is not simply

116

Lucia's, places a further query over everything else. Meanwhile the crowd was growing restless. Word had spread that the miracle was to take place at noon, and noon was past. Lucia, however, cried out suddenly 'Look at the sun!' This had become possible because the rain had ceased and the clouds had drifted aside. She herself was apparently seeing visions in the sky, but the crowd saw something quite different.

Its onset was swift but not instantaneous. Such bystanders as were within earshot duly looked at the sun. So, very soon, did many others farther away, though perhaps not all of the seventy thousand ever grasped that they were meant to. Among the large number who did look, and kept looking, there was never complete unanimity. But undoubtedly they saw something, and mass suggestion can hardly explain it, because nobody had hinted that the miracle would be solar, and when it began only a small fraction of the crowd had even heard what Lucia said.

The sun was in full view, but curiously pallid, so that it could be watched without strain – and it was moving abnormally. It traced a circle in the sky, and another, and another. It seemed to be spiralling down closer to the earth. The spectacle lasted for about eight minutes. By the end it had returned to its place and its normal brightness.

That is the basic fact, and however construed, it is a fact. I have heard an eye-witness describe it. In the absence of film we can no longer say what was objectively 'there'. Photographs taken shortly before show chiefly umbrellas. Photographs taken while the event was happening show people staring at the sky. Some of the spectators, interviewed afterwards, added more details. The sun rotated visibly, it changed colour, it shot out streamers of fire. These may have been tricks of the eye or the imagination. The terrifying downward movement was not. It caused a panic. Towards the end of the eight minutes people were shrieking, praying, grovelling, fainting. After it was over Avelino de Almeida, who

117

had come to expose a clerical fraud, wrote a graphic account for his paper. He called the sun's behaviour a 'macabre dance'. He had no idea what to make of it, but he had seen, and despite the blow to the party he supported, he was too honest a journalist to pretend otherwise.

Of the witnesses on the spot, Almeida is the most important. Another whose testimony carries weight because of its odd, backhanded character is a woman servant with a travelling English family, who described the phenomenon in a letter, yet was entirely unimpressed: this, she assumed, was something that happened in Portugal, but it was a great disappointment! Most of the other accounts are more credulous and excited. A few are by witnesses who were not actually at Fatima. Alfonso Vieira, a writer, who had taken little interest in the affair and was not on the lookout for a miracle, saw the solar motion from a place fully twenty miles away. At a school which was somewhat closer, but equally unconcerned, the spiralling sun caused an end-of-the-world scare without anyone even thinking of Fatima.

Vieira seems to have been at the limit of visibility. The director of Lisbon Observatory was interviewed and declared that his staff had recorded nothing unusual, nor could he think of any natural phenomenon that would cover the facts. Since the solar system had not been deranged, he suggested mass hallucination. The difficulty was – and is – to show how this could have been produced without preparation, could have spread through a huge crowd so rapidly, and could have taken away the faculties of unbelievers with a strong motive for resistance. Some anti-clericals who had not been present themselves tried to insist that nothing had happened, but failed to gather much support from those on the spot. The fear which prompted their insistence was justified. From 1917 onward the anti-clerical regime was declining.

Such was the Fatima miracle. There is no good expla-

118

nation of it as anything else. The trouble is that there is no good explanation of it as a miracle either.

Clearly it was nothing of a large-scale physical nature. The sun did not gyrate, nor did the earth wobble so as to make it seem to gyrate. Such aberrations would have been noticed more widely. Some freak motion of the clouds could have caused an optical illusion. Apparent solar behaviour of the same kind has been reported occasionally since, though never by a large number of observers together. But any theory has to reckon with the fact that at Fatima the event occurred on the day predicted, and roughly at the time predicted. Here physical explanations break down, or become so far-fetched as to be scarcely worth discussing.

But suppose an exception did interrupt the order of nature, through the power or influence of the Blessed Virgin. The question still remains, what exception? What happened? It can only have been a mass illusion, whether caused by freak cloud-movements or by a simultaneous interference in thousands of brains. Either way, it does not sound fitting. It sounds like a monstrous conjuring trick, inflicted on a gullible audience who took what they saw at face value.

And, granted that a higher being might do such a thing – still, what for and why thus? What did that prodigious sign really attest? The genuineness of the apparitions? There could be no point in that unless the apparitions carried a message, or presaged something to follow, as at Lourdes. In October 1917 Lucia had reported no message, only general exhortations and warnings such as might have been heard from any pulpit. There was nothing specific for the miracle to confirm. The alleged prophecy about Russia was not disclosed (if 'disclosed' is the proper word) till many years later, when the danger from Communism was a clerical cliché and had no need of Mary's belated endorsement. Lucia did mention acts of prayer and consecration which were supposed to avert the peril, but these are without interest. As for presaging any sequel at Fatima itself, the solar miracle presaged nothing. Fatima naturally became the place of pilgrimage which it still is, but no more. It never acquired any special fame for cures. The waning of the Portuguese anti-clerical party was a by-product only; the event itself had no comprehensible relation to politics.

On which unsatisfactory note, inquiry must halt. I confess to an impression that something did happen which burst the bounds of normal experience, and that it burst them more completely and bafflingly than anyone has ever been prepared to acknowledge. The solar portent does not work even *as* a miracle, in the Church's usual sense. Catholics have tried to explain it in their own way, and failed, leaving a trail of enigmas. Even to accept it as Mary's doing is surely to admit that she has an inscrutable and alarming aspect, which does not sit very well with Christian ideas of her. The answer may be yet to come. Meanwhile, no useful purpose is served by minimising the facts or trying to explain them away.

The miracles of Our Lady – medieval and modern, fictitious and (perhaps) real – bring us into the presence of something deeply distinctive. They do not come from an inscrutable Yahweh, or from a remote Godhead in what William Blake called 'the desert of the abstract'. Mary's cult has a human face, which at its best is haunting and beautiful, even when, as at Fatima, it holds a secret in reserve. There is no telling what Bernadette saw at Lourdes, or whether she physically saw anything. Psychologists claim that children can often see what is not there (the phrase is 'eidetic imagery'). Some of the other apparitions, as at Fatima, do have an air of suggestion or imitation, at least in part. But it is hard to fault Bernadette. Even Zola could not. She saw. And as she said of the Lady to a questioner afterwards, 'If you had seen her, you would have no thought or purpose which was not hers.'

Moreover, the sequel is in keeping. Superstition, commercial exploitation, clerical outrage of one sort and another – Lourdes has seen them all; and it may be that every one of its miracles can be explained away. But the healing is real, a healing of body and of spirit. There are times when silence is better than debate, and is a truer comment than any which debate could arrive at, whether proof or disproof.

At Lourdes and elsewhere in the past century and a half – let us note this again – Mary has appeared alone, and very much as a person in her own right. The ecumenical thinking of a would-be-modernised Church is hostile to this view of her. Theologians deplore the intense, almost independent personality which we have seen her acquiring in past Catholic tradition. Most of them now prefer not to think of her. If they must, they try to make her strictly part of a doctrinal scheme, a symbol rather than a person. Whether or not this is the way Christianity ought to go, it is certainly a new way, in defiance of what Our Lady had meant to many generations of Christians.

There are currents of thought outside Christianity which hint that it will not work, because, however interpreted, Mary *is* more than a symbol. She is exerting fascination today in new contexts, some of them very strange ones, and not merely as a poetic figure but as a living being who outsoars common humanity. The way she is imagined to do this varies widely. In each case some theory or school of thought has tried to claim her and fit her into its own pattern.

Theosophy, for instance, has associated her with its supposed fellowship of Adepts or Masters of Wisdom, who live on earth in secret to enlighten its peoples and guide their destinies. The early leaders of the movement – Madame Blavatsky, Annie Besant, C. W. Leadbeater – claimed to receive messages from the Masters, by telepathy or other exotic means. Among the revelations that came to Leadbeater was a report that Mary had been initiated and belonged to the fellowship. She now has an unseen benign immortality, with the wonder-working

121

powers enjoyed by her august colleagues. Theosophists and their many semi-followers have not made very much of this idea, but it is interesting that it should have arisen at all.

In the more recent heyday of Unidentified Flying Objects, beings like the Masters have reappeared in a fresh guise. They have been represented as alien visitors to Earth, vastly superior to ourselves, who created the human race or at least set it on the road to civilisation, and now hover in flying saucers keeping an eye on it. The UFO age has produced at least one Mariologist, Paul Misraki, a French artist. According to him, mankind was launched as an experiment by a Space Hierarchy. Around the beginning of the Christian era, the hierarchs gave us up in despair and decided to wipe us out, all but a select few. Jesus, who was one of the space-people, came to warn of the doom so that the few who were worthy to be saved could prepare for it, and this accounts for puzzling passages in the Gospels about an imminent end of the world. Then came a reprieve, thanks not to Jesus but to Mary. She too was one of the space-people, and about AD 50 she returned to them (the event described by Catholics as the Assumption) and persuaded them to suspend sentence. She has been acting as humanity's defence counsel ever since, interceding in the place which the Church calls heaven, and appearing at Lourdes and elsewhere to give new warnings which are not fully understood. Several kindred authors – including von Däniken, exponent of Chariots of the Gods – have explained the Fatima solar portent in UFO terms.

Meanwhile the Radical Feminist school has had its own say. Elizabeth Gould Davis, author of *The First Sex*, contends that the Marian apparitions may have been real. She gives them her own interpretation, which (like other aspects of Marian cultus) resurrects the era of Goddess-worship:

> It is an interesting fact ... that it is always the Virgin Mary who is seen in visions – never God, never the Holy Ghost,

and very rarely Jesus. The great Christian mystics to a man, and woman, claim to have seen Mary in the flesh at one time or another. . . . Those interested in psychical research may wonder whether these people actually do see something – the astral or etheric body of a real woman. But of what woman? . . . Bernadette saw her in the grotto at Lourdes and called her Mary. Who can say she is not the materialisation of a real 'Blessed Lady', the Great Goddess herself, 'the multitudin-ously named White Goddess, relic of matriarchal civilisation, or, who knows, the harbinger of its return'.

A newly-realised factor seems to be shifting the bias in outsiders' responses to Christianity. To quote another non-Christian, Gillian Tindall:

Mary, it would seem, did not die. . . . she disappeared (as she disappears from the Scriptures after her Son's death) but then she keeps reappearing. Down the ages she has ap-peared to people – at Walsingham, at Aylesford . . . at Lourdes. Jesus, we tend to feel, is dead. Whatever evangelical pamphlets may say, the image of the Crucifixion has proved too overwhelming. But Mary, it seems, lives, for many people. Strange paradox.

(*New Statesman*, May 21st 1976.)

It may not be too eccentric, then, to continue bearing the Virgin in mind, and be prepared to revert to her. Perhaps her spell is not misleading. Perhaps the thoughts which have gathered round her are authentic insights, however strangely or superstitiously expressed, and can open up a fresh line of approach to the problem of the miraculous. But before we can pursue that idea we must range wider, outside Judaism and Christianity. What about miracles in the other major religions?

6

Ambiguities in Asia

Islam is another branch from the Judaic tree. Mohammed's followers, like those of Moses and Jesus, are 'people of the Book'. Born in 570, he annexed much of the biblical tradition, and his own revelation, the Koran, is more like a huge addition to the prophetic literature of Israel – *Isaiah, Jeremiah* and so forth – than a whole new Bible in itself. His God, Allah, is the God of the Old Testament seen through Arab eyes. According to Mohammed, Allah did indeed speak to Abraham as the Bible says, but the Jews afterwards falsified the story. Israel's prophets were genuine prophets, and so was Jesus. However, the falsification was carried on and compounded. Allah chose Mohammed, 'The Prophet' *par excellence,* to sweep away the corruptions and restore the pure faith of Abraham, with enlargements to meet the needs of a greater world.

It follows that Islam, in theory, takes a biblical view of miracles. Allah works them. However, it does not give them much weight, and they have no place in the Koran comparable to their place in the Gospels. The reputed miracles of Mohammed himself are few. They rest entirely on tradition, recorded long after his death in 632, and Moslems are not bound to believe in them. Sometimes we might suspect a parody of Christian claims about miraculous proofs of Christ's authority.

The favourite proof attributed to Mohammed is grotesque. When he was in Mecca, Habib the Wise challenged him to cleave the moon in two parts. The Prophet lifted his hand towards the sky and called out to the moon to do as requested. It did a good deal better. Descending on the top of the Kaaba, Mecca's great shrine, it circled round seven times (as pilgrims are expected to do at the same spot). Then, reduced to a few inches in diameter, it flew over to the Prophet. It went up his right sleeve and down his left, entered his robe at the collar and came out at the skirt, and then – at last – broke into two. One half soared into the east of the sky, the other into the west. The challenge having thus been met, the two parts came together again and the moon was as before.

Obviously this legend is a kind of joke. The same is true of another which has become proverbial, and this too seems to reflect on Christian ideas about the miraculous proofs of Christ, even to echo his saying on the power of faith (*Matthew* 17:20). Mohammed's most famous miracle is actually a non-miracle. Once when proofs were demanded of him, he turned towards Mount Safa and ordered it to come to him. It stayed where it was. Turning back to his audience, he said: 'Allah is merciful. If it had come, it would have crushed us. I will therefore go over to it myself, and thank Allah that he has had mercy on a stiffnecked generation.' If the mountain will not come to Mohammed, evidently Mohammed must go to the mountain.

Islamic legend in general is profuse of marvels, and some of these may count as miraculous in the same sense as their Christian counterparts. Stories of healing are fairly common. The relics of holy men are said to have wonder-working properties, such as curing barrenness. However, the atmosphere of such tales is not as serious as it is for Christians. There is seldom or never contemporary evidence for them, and what is more important, Moslems do not care whether there is or not, or show much interest in establishing their truth.

The chief reason, perhaps, is that Mohammed reverted to a God who was rigorously single. The Islamic cosmos lacked the Christian complexities and nuances. Allah was awesome and remote, and had never become man. There was no Trinity and no Mother. There were no interceding saints. Hence, there was little room for a new system of the miraculous to take shape. In the mainstream of Islamic belief Allah can do anything, but his ways are too far above ours, and too arbitrary, to be examined as earthly things are examined. Story-telling is as far as humans can properly venture. While some schools of thought have built up a more elaborate theology and mythology, the spirit is unaltered. To cite one clear distinction from Christianity, Islam has its saints but has never had a canonisation procedure. Therefore the anxious sifting of testimony about miracles has never been a part of its practice.

When we move eastward into non-biblical Asia, we find radically different attitudes. Each great religion has its marvellous happenings, legendary or otherwise. But the context of ideas is so foreign to biblically-based thinking that it becomes a problem which of these happenings, if any, can be called miraculous. China, India, Tibet, having passed through their own versions of the pre-miraculous stage, all attained mental levels thousands of years ago where a natural order, with divinely ordained exceptions, seemingly might have been conceived. They had science, they had cosmic philosophies, they had gods. But the relationships were different; and so they remain. Exceptions, if they occur, cannot have the same character in Hinduism or Buddhism as in Judaism or Christianity. What character they can have, whether they ever count as miracles, whether there is common ground between oriental and western ideas, are questions demanding careful study before any answers are attempted.

Where there are gods there can, on the face of it, be miracles, as there were said to be in pagan Greece. The trouble is that the gods of Asia are not imagined in the same way. Apollo, Dionysus, Asclepius were more or less free agents and true deities. They moved in the same universe as mortals, but had a special divine place in it – Olympus – as their home, and were powerful enough to break the rules when they ranged abroad. The pre-philosophical Greek imagination was vague about anything behind them or superior to them. In the Mediter-

126

ranean world, the gods were presently replaced by the One God of the Jews and Christians, creator of the universe, who was outside and above it entirely. Asian minds also attained to the concept of a single Principle, a Supreme Being, even (in a sense) God. But this, however defined, revalued the lesser gods instead of replacing them, and was not itself sharply distinct from the universe. Asian religions do not provide for a Supreme Being who creates a system out of nothing and then intervenes in it to cause exceptions.

The Chinese alternative to creation, being less cryptic in its imagery than some others, may illustrate the Asian habit of mind. Both the traditional Chinese teachings, Confucianism and Taoism, involve an indescribable something called *Tao*. This word has been translated 'God', but misleadingly. It means a sort of inwardness, the way things are, the way things happen. Working 'in the beginning' on a cell of primeval matter, the Tao caused a split by which all the variety of nature came into being. This is the idea behind the symbolic Yin-Yang diagram, which is the basis of the I Ching or Book of Changes used in divination. Construction of the diagram starts with a circle standing for wholeness, allness, the Absolute. The Tao is represented not precisely by the circle but by the circle's perfection. Next, inside the circle, a curving line is drawn through the centre marking off equal areas of darkness and light. The dark part is negative and is Yin, the 'cold, moist, female principle', associated with earth and darkness and weight. The light or Yang is positive, the 'warm, dry, male principle', associated with sky and brightness and lightness. Neither is superior to the other. They underlie the cosmos in a union of opposites, earth and heaven. Next, inside each, a small circle of the other colour – dark within light, light within dark – shows that each contains the seeds of its opposite, and is thus unstable. Evolution can go further.

Traditional Chinese thought pursues the process along the same path. Still using the diagram as an image of it, we can say that all beings unfold from the circle and its Yin-Yang development. Their proper mode of life is the Tao which underlies all, in whatever aspect it may apply to them. In the visible order of things the Tao may sometimes be called the Way. From the basic figure the I Ching system radiates into eight further figures which stand for divisions of the universe, and sixty-four beyond those. The scheme corresponds to a theory of evolution in which the Yin and Yang generate five elements (water, fire, wood, metal, earth) and these combine in countless ways to form individual beings.

When early Chinese philosophy took up such ideas and considered the gods, it could never treat them in the naïve style of ancient Greece, as wonder-working powers answerable to nothing definite above them. They were part of the evolved system like all other beings. Philosophy looked farther, at That-of-which-they-were-a-part, and when it reached the limit of its own range it admitted nothing transcendent which could break into the system and modify it. Magic might exist, because not all the laws of the system were apparent on the surface, and a wise man could perhaps learn the more obscure ones and manipulate them to produce special effects. The gods could do likewise, after their own fashion. But no event was ever radically exceptional, eluding the system altogether, and there was no divinity Beyond to cause such events.

Confucius, who lived from 551 to 479 BC, seems to have been a down-to-earth thinker. He was mainly concerned with social morality, and he did not base this on a list of divine commandments or on any single metaphysical principle. He seldom even discussed the Tao, beyond narrow limits. For him it was chiefly 'the Way' as this applied to humanity. Virtue meant living according to it. He appealed to a past golden age when, as he believed, wise government and righteous conduct had prevailed. In view of this belief, the Tao as it actually figured in his teachings meant hardly more than the

Way of the Former Kings, which might be restored by a renewal of their wisdom. Religion was a part of this wisdom, but in a non-mystical sense. For Confucius it could almost be identified with ritual. The wise men of old were, in his eyes, 'divine sages', but they deserved the adjective because they walked closely with the gods on prescribed paths, not because they were more than human, or supernaturally inspired. There was no question of the golden age being restored by apocalyptic intervention from on high. Such an idea was alien to Confucius's mind. It may be doubted whether he would have thought of the miraculous as having any meaning at all.

At least one saying of his seems adverse to the whole notion of divine signs and significant irregularities. On a certain occasion he announced to a small group of his disciples that he was going to remain quiet. One of them asked, 'If you remain quiet, how can we ever learn anything to teach to the others?' Confucius replied, 'Does Heaven talk? The four seasons go their way in succession and the different things are produced. Does Heaven talk?'

In later Confucianism, built up round the master's teachings as an official cult, the emphasis shifted somewhat. Morality was more clearly connected with the gods. The worship of ancestors and heroes was worked into the same all-embracing scheme. Gradually the Chinese State turned its pantheon into a celestial bureaucracy, parallel to the one on earth. Furthermore, the earthly bureaucracy was the more important of the two, and the other was supposed to serve it. The Emperor had his celestial counterpart, the Jade Emperor, who headed various heavenly departments. Through the Jade Emperor and his civil service, the real Emperor and *his* civil service claimed to be able to influence the weather, avert plagues, and so forth. Countless minor deities – often deified human beings from history or legend – were appointed as the patrons of cities, crafts, professions, institutions, aspects of life. The Chinese had a kitchen god, a jewellers' god, a policemen's god, a thieves' god. All such tutelary spirits reported annually to the Jade Emperor. They were treated with courtesy in their temples, but were expected to do their jobs, and liable to be punished for failure. When rain did not fall where it was needed, the image of the local rain-spirit might be given a thrashing. In such an atmosphere, divinity had a non-western meaning. It was not only a part of the system but an auxiliary rather than a governing part. While all this was a long way from the cool and practical Confucius, the western idea of the miraculous remained excluded.

Taoism, the other native Chinese religion, was founded by Lao Tzu. His life overlapped Confucius's and they are said to have met. His teaching took up the Tao in a more mystical and impersonal spirit, stressing it as the inscrutable Nature-of-Things. From it, he said, came the secret essence of every being. Wisdom and strength could be achieved by attunement to it, without thought or effort. For him the Tao was not ultimate. There was a mysterious abyss of Non-Being behind it, from which it arose. However, he did not envisage an active power outside the system, any more than Confucius did. His universe had more scope for the wayward but still none for the miraculous.

The Taoist movement which claimed him as its founder was anti-Confucian. It drew on his single cryptic book to justify a revolt against rules, a holy anarchism. It was for rebels, artists, adventurers. Besides a general do-what-you-will atmosphere, including group sex and a cult of wine, it promoted magic. A series of Taoist sages built up a school of alchemy, with much talk of the elixir of life. Some of them claimed that they actually were immortal. When they seemed to die, their followers spread reports that the grave was empty and had only personal oddments in it, such as clothes or a cane. Other Taoists wrote about the making of gold, like western alchemists.

But it was done in disregard of any such notion as the

miraculous. Taoists searched for formulae and techniques, however bizarre. Unlike Confucians they favoured experimental science. Several of the best-known Chinese inventions – the compass, gunpowder, porcelain, various dyes and medicines, acupuncture – are ascribed to them. Early in the Christian era, their magic itself was schematised as a kind of science, combining alchemy with dietary and breathing techniques, and with a theory that human beings had thousands of tiny gods inside them, who could be organised as a team in the interests of bodily and mental health. This last notion was an individualised version of China's divine bureaucracy. It too implied built-in deities who served mankind in an orderly manner, rather than looking down from above and subverting its accustomed life-styles.

India – Hindu India, that is – abounds in the marvellous more than any other country. During the last century, its abundance has spilt over into Europe and America. Much of the revival of occultism and magic has been due to Wisdom-of-the-East zealots such as Madame Blavatsky, foundress of Theosophy, who have studied Hinduism and placed their own constructions upon it. However, the first step here is to sweep nearly all Hindu wonder-working aside, not as being fictitious, but as being unmiraculous.

Thus yogis claim to do bodily feats which an outsider might judge to be superhuman. They can live for weeks without nourishment, endure fantastic extremes of heat and cold, go into suspended animation, stop breathing (or nearly so) for hours, change their rate of heartbeat. Some of these claims, the last two for instance, have stood up to laboratory testing. Others are more doubtful. But even if they are all valid, the feats depend on psychosomatic techniques and are done at will. A yogi would never pretend that they were miracles. In fact it would take away from his self-esteem if they were.

Other Hindu thaumaturgy is simply conjuring, aided

131

by hypnotic patter. After much debate this seems to have emerged as the probable truth about the rope trick. What is said to happen, or appear to happen, is that the conjurer gathers a circle of spectators and sits in the middle with a small boy beside him. He takes a rope out of a basket and throws one end up into the air. It stiffens like a pole. The boy climbs it and vanishes. The conjurer climbs up after him with a long knife, slashes about in the air, and brings down dismembered portions of the boy, which he piles on the ground and covers with a cloth. Then the rope falls and the boy crawls out from under the cloth, unharmed and smiling.

For a long time the standard explanation was that the trick was a traveller's tale which always came at second-hand. 'You never meet anybody who has actually seen it.' However, there is now at least one eye-witness account by a western observer. John Taussig, a journalist and ex-army intelligence officer, saw the trick performed at the village of Premnagar near Dehra Dun. At the time he was baffled. Still, he noticed a fact omitted from previous reports – that the conjurer talked without a pause, giving a running commentary on everything he (apparently) did. Later Taussig saw a variant of the trick in Delhi, where the conjurer cut up a little girl and threw her tongue to a dog to eat, after which she reappeared in one piece. Again the descriptive patter, in Hindustani, was incessant. This time a bystander gave Taussig a clue. He asked what the conjurer was supposed to be doing, since he only talked on and on without action. When Taussig described the trick, he protested that he had seen no trick, and no dog, either. The difference between the bystander and Taussig was that the former had no Hindustani and did not know what the conjurer was saying. In other words the rope trick and its variants are done by spell-binding mass suggestion, which fails with an onlooker who does not know the language, or does not know it well enough to be spellbound. That is why Europeans seldom see the rope trick. They only see a conjurer chattering and cannot follow him. Which is all very extraordinary, and might even be thought magical after its fashion, but has nothing to do with miracles.

When we turn from such expendable items, and look for the miraculous in serious Hindu thought, we move on to tricky ground. We find, as in China, the recurring Asian idea of a single Something from which all things evolve, including the gods. In India this is called Brahman. If it were simply the evolving Tao under another name, there would, as in China, be nothing 'outside', so Hindiusm could have no concept of the miraculous. But the pattern is different. In the upshot it is hard to be precise at all.

To begin with, though Brahman cannot be equated with God, it has a God-aspect. This can be worshipped and communed with, and is often represented by the deity Vishnu. Secondly, the world we see and experience is nothing like the whole of the evolved reality. It is only a realm of appearances, and even, in a sense, a realm of illusion. The deeper nature of things is veiled, in an unmanifest Beyond. That is where true causation lies, not in the causes known to science and common sense. For instance, a man may think that the shape of his life is moulded by his upbringing, the place where he lives, the job he chooses, the people he meets, and so forth . . . but he deceives himself. It is really the result of his conduct in previous lives, and obeys what is called the law of karma. That law is simply affirmed; it cannot be investigated like, say, the law of gravity, because it functions outside the manifest world.

It might be thought that the Beyond resembled the Christian heaven in the sense of harbouring miracle-causing agencies. That would be a mistake. Hinduism, indeed, has a rich tradition of superior beings who can work wonders that are more than mere conjuring tricks. Such are the legendary sages called rishis, and the more advanced yogis, who profess even today that they can (for example) levitate. But they all do it themselves, by passing through the veil of appearances and mastering

133

the higher laws of the unmanifest. Prolonged self-discipline, fasting, concentration, are supposed to give the power to do this in a more or less automatic way. Most Hindu wonder-working is really pictured as a metaphysical species of magic. The Beyond is passive, impersonal. There is nothing in it that takes a hand or intervenes. In human life, moreover, any real exceptions would be against the grain of the law of karma. It has been alleged that the frequent Hindu addiction to gambling is due to a belief that there is no other way of cracking karma's iron regularity. Blind chance may divert the course of one's fate, it is no use hoping that anything else will, certainly not a miracle.

Gods in general are part of the same system as mortals, and subject to similar laws. A question does arise over the cult of Vishnu as Supreme Being, in a different class altogether. His worshippers maintain that he has sometimes taken human form. The most famous of his earthly visits was in the guise known as Krishna. The popular Krishna saga includes amazing feats which he simply performs, like Christ, in virtue of his divinity and with no technique leading up to them. They are open, at least, to that interpretation. One of them is the opposite of Joshua's solar standstill: he creates a false sunset during a battle, to confuse the army his friends are fighting. Krishna perhaps may be said to have worked true miracles – in legend, that is – whereas the lesser gods and the rishis do not.

However, serious Hindu thinking would not view the distinction as important, or spend much time on the precise anatomy of the marvellous. While Hindus and Christians may differ here, the wiser sort in both religions have a likeness of attitude which should not go unnoticed. The Hindus echo such saints as Teresa of Avila. They acknowledge the marvellous, but refuse to lay the chief emphasis on it. If you make spiritual progress, you may become able to perform quasi-miracles, or (in Christian terms) miracles may happen for you. But if you treat them as more than by-products, and try

134

to cultivate your supposed gift, you are getting side-tracked into error. They are not what matters. It is the spiritual progress itself that matters. If thaumaturgy distracts you from that, it can be dropped without loss, and should be.

In the 1920s, when Mahatma Gandhi was adored to the point of near-deification by his followers, many believed he had superhuman powers. He sternly discouraged them, not only because he denied having such powers, but because he judged the belief itself to be pernicious. Thus, a rumour spread that the British authorities could never suppress him, because, if they arrested him, he would fly out of the window. When they did arrest him, and he did not fly out of the window, he remarked that it was a good thing for his movement. Indians would now learn to act for themselves instead of putting their trust in a wonder-working Mahatma. A few years later he was on a train journey when people started shouting that he had worked a miracle. Another passenger had fallen out on his head, but was unhurt. Gandhi told the man not to be silly: 'If I'd had anything to do with it, I wouldn't have let you fall.'

With Gandhi it was a matter of plain denial. A more profound story is told of Buddha, who began as a Hindu reformer rather than the inventor of a new religion. He once came to a river and was informed that a famous yogi lived on its bank. For twenty years this yogi had put himself through agonies of fasting and penance, and now claimed that he could walk on the surface of the river, clear across to the other side. Buddha said: 'What a waste of effort, when he could cross by the ferry for a small coin.'

7

Thinking Makes It So

Buddhism, the religion based on Buddha's teachings, moved a long way from its origins. In its Indian home-land it very nearly expired. In the countries where it found a footing, it became something much more indi-vidual than a mere Hindu reform. The process reached an apex of strangeness and complexity in Tibet, where it mingled with older native cults dominated by shamans or wizards. Under the auspices of the 'lama' priesthood Tibet became a theocracy ruled by the Dalai Lama. Buddhism of the same type spread to Mongolia. It re-vived the wonder-working tradition of the Indian home-land, with more besides. In theory it denied the miraculous, in practice it came close to admitting it, in a peculiar sense which no other religion has defined.

Despite Communist conquests, Lamaistic Buddhism is not dead, and it can still be properly spoken of in the present tense. The lamas, like the teachers of Hinduism, speak of a Beyond transcending the world we know by the senses, and more important. But they give it an un-Hindu positiveness. It is a kind of infinite mind-energy underlying appearances. As the western scholar Evans-Wentz puts it, matter itself is held to be a development of thought, 'crystallised mental energy'. While this mental Beyond has a basic unity, it is not thought of as a single God but as a hierarchy of beings who have an indescribable nature between crude reality and symbol. They exist, but not quite as humans exist. They include a medley of gods, ranging from *yidams*, the tutelary spirits of individuals, to august primal entities who pre-side over epochs of the cosmos. Lamaism has also ab-sorbed an Indian mystique of sex, and artists portray the higher beings with *shaktis*, female partners who (so to speak) activate them.

In a scheme of things where Mind is the arch-reality, we might expect a great deal to be made of mental powers. This is so. Lamas claim to do all sorts of extraordinary things through mind-energy and concentration. They reject the miraculous on the ground that all phenomena are governed by laws, even though they may not be laws that meet the eye, and the human wonder-worker does it himself by understanding them. This is more or less the Hindu position. However, as we shall see, there are further affirmations which call it in question.

In the first half of the twentieth century, when Lamaistic Buddhism was still at its height, and the countries where it flourished became – for a time – not too difficult to reach, several travellers from the west reported on its lore of marvels. One of the most distinguished was Alexandra David-Neel, a French convert to Buddhism, author of *With Mystics and Magicians in Tibet*. Most of her work was done in the second and third decades of the century. Thanks to her and others, we have some fascinating accounts of the lamas' feats or alleged feats, and the theories behind them. Some are part of semi-legendary tradition, others relate to the present.

One much-loved story tells how the Mongol emperor Kublai Khan invited priests of all religions into his presence. Each urged the claims of his own creed, except for a lama, who simply advised Kublai to ask for a practical demonstration. When Kublai at last did so, none of them took up the challenge. He then asked the lama himself. The lama looked steadily at the emperor, and a goblet of wine rose from the table to Kublai's lips. He confessed the superiority of Buddhism.

This does not sound like a true miracle, nor is it asserted to be so. On lamaistic assumptions there was no special divine action, and the event was not even an exception to the laws of the universe. Supposedly at least, the thing was done by a mind-power technique which initiates of the true faith can master. In much the same spirit are the claims of modern lamas about the

137

startling results of Tibetan versions of yoga – astral travelling, teleportation, imperviousness to cold. Some of these can be matched in the occult lore of other countries. Some are more original, such as the ability to lighten the body to a point where an adept can walk in giant strides, at thirty or forty miles an hour (Mme David-Neel said she had seen this done).

Lamas insist, not only that such feats are unmiraculous, but that they are morally neutral. A Christian saint and a Tibetan hermit may both levitate, but it is only seen as a proof of holiness in the case of the former. To the claim that Christ worked miracles at will, and that these prove his unique character and spiritual greatness, a lama would retort (*a*) that they were not miracles, (*b*) that others, with practice, can do the same, and (*c*) that they prove nothing about spiritual greatness, being within the power of evil thaumaturgists as well as good ones. No divine irruption from the Beyond is implied.

Alexandra David-Neel, however, describes a procedure in which such irruptions do seem to happen. Although they are explained away, the explaining-away opens up another field of Tibetan thought where distinctions become blurred. Here at least among the great religions of Asia, we find the idea of the miraculous creeping in despite the denials, even though it takes an alien form.

The procedure described is used in teaching junior lamas. The master instructs the novice to retire into a hermitage and invite his *yidam*, his tutelary god, to appear. This invitation must be more than a prayer. He must concentrate, meditate, go through spiritual exercises. His efforts may be fruitless, but if he succeeds, the *yidam* finally shows itself. At first it is simply an image standing in front of him. But with perseverance it comes to life, grows more definite, moves about. By a supreme effort he may induce it to come outside his cell. When that hurdle has been cleared, it is a companion he can evoke at will. The master congratulates him. Should

138

he now wish to go, he can go in triumph, with the *yidam* as his guardian angel.

If he does, however, the master is disappointed. A truly successful student remains unsatisfied, and progresses further by what appears to be a retreat. He becomes convinced that the *yidam* is not a god distinct from himself but a creature of his own mind. The master tries to reassure him. He sinks, however, into a pit of despair, and confesses that although the *yidam* is still with him, he cannot believe in its independent reality. He has projected it from himself. Then the master makes his real point. 'You are right. You have grasped what you were meant to grasp. Gods, demons, the whole universe, are but a mirage which exists in the mind, "springs from it, and sinks into it".'

The question is, whose mind? Presumably 'the whole universe' springs from the one Universal Mind, the boundless mental energy which crystallises as matter. But what about the *yidam*? It is not just a hallucination. In defiance of the habitual course of nature, it comes out of empty air and is actually present. Lamaistic teaching gives the fact a much wider application. With training, it suggests, an adept can create from his own individual mind, making his own little interpolations in the natural order. Thoughts have reality, and a thought-form can have substance. The Tibetan word is *tulpa.*

We need, first, to grasp exactly what is said about *tulpas*, and then to consider what it really implies. An adept can create many things besides mini-gods. He can form a copy of himself, a doppelganger. He can form another person, an animal, a physical object. Such *tulpas* are composed of a kind of temporary matter distilled from mind-energy. They are not 'there' as ordinary matter is 'there', but if they are strongly projected and maintained, other people can see them. Sometimes they can acquire enough tangibility to be felt as well. In the tale of Gesar, an ancient epic popular in Tibet and Mongolia, the hero is a master of the art of *tulpa*-projection and uses it in battle. Gesar's enemies are be-

139

wildered by phantasms of himself in different places, and by phantasmal soldiers, horses and tents. Such optical tricks occur also in Hindu legend, but these are more. The *tulpa* tents give shelter. The *tulpa* horses can be ridden. The *tulpa* soldiers kill enemies with *tulpa* weapons.

This of course is heroic legend. But similar if more modest feats have been reported in the twentieth century. In 1923 the Tashi or Panchen Lama was in danger from his political opponents. He escaped from his monastery at Shigatse leaving a thought-form of himself behind which, it is reputed, behaved as he would have done, deceived everybody till he had travelled to a safe distance, and then vanished. Mme David-Neel describes a public occasion when a lama stepped out of the sedan chair he was riding in, walked up to a statue, and simply faded into it. His chair was found to be empty. The numerous witnesses had apparently seen a thought-form of the lama, who had never been there at all. Even if such an event is a mass illusion we have the same sort of problem as at Fatima. Without prior suggestion or hypnosis, the mass illusion is a mystery in itself. In 1912 the Dalai Lama told Mme David-Neel that the powers of a sufficiently advanced being – a Bodhisattva, in Buddhist parlance – are almost without limit. Not only can he appear in many places at once, and scatter phantasmal people about the landscape; he can create 'hills, enclosures, houses, forests, roads, bridges', and affect the weather.

A further development is the *tulku*. Under certain conditions, a *tulpa* can be so stable and solid as to be indistinguishable from normal reality. Given a special focusing of thought and will – by a superior being, or by several people together – a human *tulpa* can result which is an actual person, able to live a complete life from conception to death. Such a person is born in the usual way and is called a *tulku* or 'phantom body'. A *tulku* child need not be visibly different from other children, but embodies a god, or a demon, or someone who has lived before, or perhaps simply a hope or ideal – whatever it was that the creator or creators may have been thinking about. This is the clue to such puzzling notions as the mystic succession of Dalai Lamas. Each may develop quite differently from his predecessors, yet they are all the same person, because they are all *tulkus* of the same personality-pattern, which is conserved from generation to generation and transcends the accidents of life. When a Dalai Lama dies, a search is made for the *tulku* child born soon after who can be recognised as bearing the same stamp. (It remains to be seen whether this custom will survive the Chinese conquest of Tibet.)

Stated thus, the theory of *tulpas* and *tulkus* still suggests magic rather than miracles. A thought-form may be an anomaly in nature, but it is not tossed in by an inscrutable agency Beyond, it is made by conscious technique, however weird. That, surely, is the moral of the *yidam* exercise? But although lamas officially take this line, they also make admissions which reveal the matter to be more complex. Individual will and imagination, whether exerted singly or pooled, are not the whole story. Thought-forms in some degree elude both. They can, it seems, appear spontaneously without being willed at all. They can change, growing away from the concept that gave them birth. They can turn against their creators: legends tell of adepts whose *tulpas* turned into Frankenstein monsters and attacked them. They can roam away on their own, out of the adept's control and knowledge. They can remain active after his death, doing things he never intended. Also, when they are produced jointly (as in the case of a *tulku*), the thoughts of all the people involved can hardly coincide in detail; so a factor which is not in their own minds must be giving coherence and unity to the creation that results.

On the lamas' own showing, something from Beyond enters into the process, something humanly incalculable. The creator of thought-forms is not supplying all the materials himself. Rather he is attuning himself

141

to the Universal Mind, using his own energies to tap and release its greater ones. In the *yidam* exercise, when the novice-master tells his pupil that the mind creates everything, he obviously does not mean that the puny individual ego creates everything. His lesson is that the Universal Mind is the source of all, and the student is a part of it, has achieved a degree of identification with it, is acting in the same way. In a sense both are right, the student who completes the course, and his less advanced colleague who believes naïvely in the *yidam*'s reality. The world, with 'all things visible and invisible', is projected by the One Mind. While gods exist, they are not strictly outside yourself because, at the deepest level, you and the One Mind are united.

Nevertheless, the One Mind is a great deal more than your own ego. In the lore of *tulpas* and *tulkus* the phenomena, though partly under the adept's control, are not entirely so. Something comes from Beyond, something unpredictable, something other. The happenings may be unlike Christian miracles in their spirit and atmosphere, but they are not so unlike in their supposed nature.

Furthermore, the lamaistic sect which gives most prominence to thought-forms also regards the Beyond as having a headquarters in a sort of heaven aloof from mankind. The sect is called Kalachakra, 'the Wheel of Time', and it claims an origin in a place called Shambhala, where the Beyond and the world we know overlap. Shambhala's mythos is copious; the only point here is that Lamaism does have this counterpart of the Christian heaven under the aspect we are concerned with – heaven as a source of divine power and wonderworking, distinct from the realm of normal experience.

The full name of this mysterious place is Chang Shambhala, 'North' Shambhala. Traditions which carry weight seem to put it in a higher latitude than Tibet and most of Mongolia, perhaps among the Altai mountains. It is a hidden citadel in a natural fastness, not to be reached except by those mystically summoned. Its inhabitants are more than human, and its divine kings have an occult influence over the affairs of humanity. Buddha himself went there to be initiated into the deepest wisdom. Secret messages and signs emanate from Shambhala to guide chosen agents among mankind. The fastness in the Altai mountains (or wherever it is) is not the whole of Shambhala, which is heavenly as well as earthly. The rays of its heavenly portion can sometimes be seen lighting the northern sky. In the words of a western traveller, Shambhala is 'the Holy Place, where the earthly world links with the highest states of consciousness'. Some of the greatest wonder-workers and *tulpa*-creators, the epic hero Gesar for instance, are associated with it, and, in one phase or another of their lives, empowered by it.

The traveller just quoted is Nicholas Roerich, who was gathering data on Lamaistic Buddhism at about the same time as Mme David-Neel. Roerich was a Russian artist and anthropologist of immense talent. He supplied Stravinsky with the background material for *The Rite of Spring*. From 1923 to '28 he was leading a leisurely expedition through Central Asia, accompanied by his son, a scientist of a more academic type. Besides much painting and field-work in anthropology, Roerich investigated Shambhala and allied topics. He believed in it himself. Or at least, he believed in a reality underlying the legend. He seems to have thought that he was receiving messages from Shambhala and that his work was a mission on its behalf.

In the 1920s both he and Mme David-Neel found Shambhala to be a living issue in Central Asia. It was the focus of a revolutionary mystique, an early stirring of Asian nationalism. This had an apocalyptic tone, recalling the hopes of naïve Christians about the Second Coming of Christ out of heaven. The divine king of Shambhala was going to emerge and lead a Buddhist holy war against western imperialists. In Tibet the Tashi Lama, who was second in status to the Dalai Lama, became so deeply involved that political pressure

143

forced him to leave. He travelled through Mongol country founding colleges of Kalachakra, which were asserted to be in touch with Shambhala. Mongols identified the promised saviour with the hero Gesar, who would be reborn in the sacred stronghold to head the imminent crusade.

Thought-forms played a notable part in the folklore of this movement. The Tashi Lama's freedom to take a lead in it was a consequence of his *tulpa* powers: this was the time when he outwitted his enemies by creating a phantasm of himself, which impersonated him at Shigatse till he was over the border. A lama told Mme David-Neel that the Messiah, Gesar-come-again, would be 'constructed' by the united thoughts of the Mongolian people. 'He will be the *tulku* of all of us whom the foreigners wish to make their slaves.' Here quite plainly is the idea of a vague collective thought being given substance through a partnership with a higher realm. Earthly yearning is to be fulfilled by heaven, or, at any rate, by Shambhala, not solely by the unfocused mind-energies of those who yearn. We have at least a faint echo of a more familiar theme – God sending a Messiah in fulfilment of Jews' Messianic hopes.

Tulpas are not purely oriental hearsay. Westerners have made their acquaintance. Even today Kalachakra survives in Mongolia, and at least one living Englishman (whom I have met) was initiated there and has made thought-form experiments. These must be left to him to describe, should he elect to do so. But another experiment is public property. Alexandra David-Neel performed it herself and recorded it in her book. It seems not only to prove that thought-forms are possible, but to bear out the inference that there is more to them than the thoughts of their creators.

She began by composing a mental image of a Tibetan monk, 'short and fat, of an innocent and jolly type'. Having pictured him, she went through a prescribed course of concentration and ritual. Months passed.

Then the image appeared before her. It soon vanished, but after a while she was able to summon it again. Her monk looked real, and she found that without her giving conscious attention to detail, he was consistent. She always saw the same man, not a wavering figment.

About this time she resumed her travels, on horseback, with a few Tibetan companions. On the road she began seeing the monk whether she was thinking of him or not. He behaved like a real person, walking beside her horse, and stopping from time to time to look round, without being willed to. Occasionally he touched her, very lightly. Then at last he did start changing, but not because of any change in her mental picture. An obscure process was turning him into a quasi-person in his own right. He was breaking free from her conception, becoming thinner and less genial-looking. Also, though she had kept all this to herself and never spoken of her monk, other people were catching glimpses of him. Deciding to make an end, she willed him to disappear. He took no notice. For six months she was fighting against her own stubborn thought-form. Again and again he came back. She could only cancel him by a sustained effort of concentration, like the effort which had first called him into being.

Two 'rational' explanations come to mind. While each of them covers part of the story, each is refuted by another part. She might have suggested herself into a long-drawn hallucination, which slowly changed for subconscious reasons – perhaps because of memories of a real monk, who had some significance for her and whom the image grew to resemble. But if so, how did her companions see the figure as well? On the other hand she might have suggested them into seeing it by a hypnotic patter, as in the Indian rope trick. But that idea conflicts with the nature of her own vision, with her silence about it, with her displeasure that anyone else should be involved.

Obviously Mme David-Neel may have made it all up, though there is no evident reason to distrust her. Even that method of disposal fails to dispose of Nicholas Roerich, who tells a more startling *tulpa* story. At least, that is what it appears to be, and it is startling on more counts than one. It occurs in his travel diary, published under the title *Altai-Himalaya*, describing his expedition through Central Asia. In the summer of 1927 he was encamped with his party in the Shara-gol valley, a little-known tract between Mongolia and Tibet. Engrossed in his reveries about Shambhala, he built a shrine dedicated to that elusive centre. It was finished early in August, and a number of lamas gathered from the surrounding country for the ceremony of consecration. At this point Roerich's diary has the following entry:

> On August fifth – something remarkable! We were in our camp in the Kukunor district not far from the Humboldt Chain. In the morning about half past nine some of our caravaneers noticed a remarkably big black eagle flying over us. Seven of us began to watch this unusual bird. At this same moment another of our caravaneers remarked, 'There is something far above the bird.' And he shouted in his astonishment. We all saw, in a direction from north to south, something big and shiny reflecting the sun, like a huge oval moving at great speed. Crossing our camp the thing changed in its direction from south to southwest. And we saw how it disappeared in the intense blue sky. We even had time to take out field glasses and saw quite distinctly an oval form with shiny surface, one side of which was brilliant from the sun.

In another book, *Himalayas, Abode of Light*, Roerich recorded the incident again.

> A sunny, unclouded morning – the blue sky is brilliant. Over our camp flies a huge, dark vulture. Our Mongols and we watch it. Suddenly one of the Buriat lamas points into the blue sky. 'What is that? A white balloon? An aeroplane?' – We notice something shiny, flying very high from the north-east to the south. We bring three powerful field glasses from the tents and watch the huge spheroid body shining against the sun, clearly visible against the blue sky and moving very fast. Afterwards we see that it sharply changes its direction from south to southwest and disappears behind the snow-peaked Humboldt Chain.

146

This second version adds a few details to the first. The sky was cloudless. They went to their tents to fetch the binoculars – therefore, although the object was travelling fast, they had time to do that. Also, the change of flight-direction was sharp.

The outstanding and piquant fact is that this incident is a classic 'flying saucer' sighting twenty years in advance of the main UFO wave, which began to roll in June 1947. The object, it seems, was a shining oval with a degree of convexity. It rode through the air with nothing to show what drove it, or what held it up. It moved swiftly, more or less in a straight line, and then made an abrupt turn. These are characteristics of flying saucers. There are common-sense explanations which are supposed to account for such things, and in general they do, but none will account for this one. It was not a cloud. Nor was it a weather balloon or satellite – not in Central Asia in 1927. Nor was it a product of suggestion. Modern UFO-seeing may well be largely that, because modern UFO-seers have already got the idea in their heads. But in 1927 nobody had. Even if Roerich invented the entire story, trusting that none of his companions would contradict him, it is still very hard to see how he came to invent a flying saucer twenty years before they were first reported.

Granted that Roerich (and presumably the rest of his party) saw something, what was it? One at least of the anti-UFO arguments does apply. Unbelievers insist, rightly, that flying saucers cannot be manned vehicles or even physical objects at all, because they fly quickly in a straight line and then turn sharply. No machine could carry out such a manoeuvre, and even if a sharp turn could somehow be made, the crew would be flung forward in their cabin and killed. Since Roerich's oval did fly quickly, and turn sharply, it was not a flying machine. Its motion defied the normal laws of mechanics.

Clearly, in fact, the story has a psychological aspect. It cannot be detached from what Roerich was doing at

147

the time. He was thinking about Shambhala; he and his companions had just been putting up a Shambhalic shrine; and out of the north, where Shambhala was supposed to lie, the portent appeared. Yet the strange parallel with later UFO descriptions (however we interpret those) forbids its dismissal as a mere group-hallucination brought on by mystical fantasies. How did people in 1927 manage to hallucinate that? Nothing in Buddhist art or myth could have led them to expect it. Bizarre as the inference may be, it seems as if this Un-identified Flying Object may actually have been a structure of thought-made-visible, a *tulpa*, taking a form which UFO experience has since shown to correspond to some pattern in the human mind. Shambhala, moreover, was the reputed home of those very myths and doctrines which laid most stress on the *tulpa* motif. The setting and atmosphere were both right for a thought-form to appear, and it did.

In the book which gives the second account, Roerich says that lamas who saw the object with him called it 'the sign of Shambhala'. He also records a discussion with another lama, who had not been there himself, but professed to recognise the type of event. This one said to him:

'You are guarded by Shambhala. The huge black vulture is your enemy, who is eager to destroy your work, but the protecting force from Shambhala follows you in this Radiant form of Matter. This force is always near you but you cannot always perceive it. Sometimes only, it is manifested for strengthening and directing you. Did you notice the direction in which this sphere moved? You must follow the same direction ... You must know and realise the manner in which people are helped because often people repel the help which is sent.'

'Manifestation' in a 'radiant form of matter' certainly refers to the *tulpa* idea. The lama, however, did not regard the flying oval as created by the thoughts of Roerich himself or of his party collectively. The shrine was only the occasion of its appearing. Its origin was

148

from someone or something in Shambhala. And while an earthly Shambhala was believed to exist, as a college of adepts concealed (possibly) in the Altai mountains, this same lama emphasised that it was heavenly also, being indeed 'the Holy Place', as Roerich phrased it himself, 'where the earthly world links with the highest states of consciousness'. Shambhala, apparently, is at least as much in the Beyond as it is here.

To sum up: the object in the sky behaved as no material thing could, and according to the lamas it came as an intervention of Mind from Beyond, occasioned by attuned earthly minds, and sent as a sign. However alien the language and imagery, we confront an event which is in much the same style as the miracles attendant on Christian saints and seers. The way it happened recalls (for instance) the solar portent at Fatima.

Since parallels of a sort have begun to emerge, it is worth asking whether these lamaistic ideas can shed any light on problems which have perplexed westerners. For instance, do they suggest a fresh way of looking at the miracles in the Gospels?

We must be on guard against imagining that *tulpas* or *tulkus* are going to 'explain' them. It would be no use getting caught in another old-fashioned and misleading attempt to rationalise. In any case, this would hardly count as rationalising. Christian mysteries are not to be disposed of by substituting Tibetan ones. The point, rather, is to ask whether any of the miracle-stories sound enough like *tulpa*-stories to suggest a kindred tradition at work: one which inspired them, or affected them, or literally entered into the actions of Christ, according to how far we regard the Gospels as history. To trace a likeness need not detract from him, or conflict with Christian orthodoxy. It need not do what Wisdom-of-the-East enthusiasts have so often tried to do – turn him into a kind of guru. In lamaistic terms, we could say that he was the unique man who had mastery in the divine Beyond and could produce thought-forms in-

149

stantly at will. That would be compatible with the Incarnation. God, the supreme Mind, has mastery in the divine Beyond; so, therefore, has God-made-man.

The scope, however, is limited. The Virgin Birth might be construed as the formation of a unique *tulku* in Mary's womb, corresponding to God's will and human Messianic hopes. A few of the miracles Christ performs during his ministry awaken faint echoes. When he multiplies the loaves so as to feed five thousand people, it vaguely recalls the wonder-working of Gesar. That Tibetan hero creates hosts of *tulpa* soldiers solid enough to kill his enemies. Likewise, *tulpa* bread would doubtless be solid enough to satisfy hunger. If the same story were told in a Tibetan setting, that is how we would be expected to understand it. In the New Testament, however, no such meaning comes naturally to mind, because most of the other miracles are quite different. Not enough of them resemble the Feeding of the Five Thousand to suggest a general conception at work.

The *tulpa* notion becomes more interesting when we turn to the Resurrection. The risen Christ is by no means merely the flesh-and-blood Jesus resuscitated. He is that, but he is more, and mysterious. His appearance varies, so that friends and disciples, Mary Magdalene for instance, fail to recognise him at once. He passes through closed doors. He vanishes in Jerusalem, is seen in Galilee, vanishes there and is seen in Jerusalem again, and finally 'ascends' out of sight, passing into some other mode of being. The reports insist on his physical reality – he can eat, and the sceptical Thomas can feel his wounds – but his body has changed. It does behave like a *tulpa*. It could be composed of what Roerich's lama called the radiant form of matter, mind-substance.

There we might halt, judging, at most, that the Resurrection stories may have been influenced by some ancient lore which surfaces in Lamaism as well. But one datum forces us to go further. This is the Holy Shroud of Turin. As we saw, while the image on it has often been

150

denounced as a fake, nobody has explained how the fake could have been carried out, how such an image could have been stamped on the cloth. Experiment has shown, on the other hand, that the image might have been formed by a human body if something extraordinary happened to it, releasing a burst of radiation. Was the corpse transfigured – truly, literally transfigured – into a glorified living substance which the lamas' beliefs obscurely hint at? And do the Resurrection stories reflect that substance's *tulpa* properties?

Having taken note of such an astounding possibility, we can only leave it and pass on. There is little to pass on to. Christian hagiographic lore still has few points of contact with *tulpa* theory. Thought-forms might be invoked in cases of bilocation by saints, and in such legends as that of Our Lady creating an apparition to take the place of the runaway nun. But Christian stories which can be construed thus are not very common. In modern times, a vague kinship is evident between the Fatima portent and Roerich's UFO, yet it does not seem possible to do much more than say so.

Fatima, however, raises a further issue. UFO theorists have tried to annex it, claiming that what the Portuguese crowd really saw was a flying saucer. The idea is far-fetched even by the standards of UFO theorists. Descriptions of the solar movement are not much like the flying saucer reports of later years. On the other hand, Roerich's description of his Shambhalic thought-form (if that is how we should regard it) foreshadows them very closely, so closely that accident seems out of the question. Thought-forms may not be of much help with Christian miracles, apart perhaps from the central and supreme one, but can they help – and if so, to what effect regarding the miraculous – with recognised problems outside religion? Consider flying saucers: could it be that this is just what some of them are?

Not all, of course, or even a large proportion. The majority of flying saucers can be safely forgotten. They

151

are clouds or satellites or weather balloons or optical illusions . . . or hoaxes. However, a few survive critical scrutiny. It is at least interesting that Roerich's, the forerunner of the rest, should have appeared exactly where the *tulpa* doctrine was ready to hand as an explanation. Could the others also be *tulpas*, projected world-wide by some unknown agency extending its activities beyond Central Asia? Or for that matter, could they be unintentional *tulpas* produced independently by people whose minds harbour such an image? This view, indeed, is very much what C. G. Jung suggested in his book on them, though it appears that he did not know about *tulpas*, and hit on the idea himself.

It goes without saying that thought-forms may be relevant to some of the hardy annuals of psychical research – ghosts, phantasms of the living, and so forth. Rather than wander off into such obvious but dubious fields, we might reflect more intriguingly on a topic which is less obvious: their possible bearing on another problem now confessed to be real, the evidence in support of natal astrology.

This was amassed in the early 1970s by Michel and Françoise Gauquelin. Their case convinced Professor H. P. Eysenck, whose article 'Planets, Stars and Personality' (*New Behaviour*, May 29th, 1975) was the first easily accessible summary of it in English. It leads to what seems a total impasse, which thought-form theory might resolve.

The Gauquelins made lists of successful scientists, actors and sportsmen. The test of success was objective, being simply whether the person had been made the subject of a biography. On this basis they collected 3,647 in the first group, 1,409 in the second, and 1,553 in the third. They then chose a suitable planet for each class of person, and determined its position at the birth of each member of the class. Saturn was assigned to the scientists, Jupiter to the actors, Mars to the sports champions. In each class the Gauquelins found a marked correlation with the behaviour of the planet. The proportion of scientists born soon after Saturn rose, and soon after it had reached its highest point in the sky, turned out to be so far above random expectation that it would be perverse to dismiss the result as chance. The same happened with the actors in relation to Jupiter, and with the sportsmen in relation to Mars. When the Gauquelins announced their findings, a sceptical scientific committee repeated the test by picking a fresh sample of 535 Belgian sportsmen and trying them as well. This list showed a similar pattern.

Astrology therefore seemed to have scored a triumph. A very limited triumph – there was still nothing to favour conventional horoscope-casting based on the Zodiac – but a triumph none the less. The trouble was, as Professor Eysenck pointed out in his re-telling, that no causal link could be traced, or even plausibly guessed at. That is still the trouble. The correlations are clear, but they make no sense. When astrology was invented, the planets were considered to be the abodes of gods, and their influence was explained in that way. Gods, after all, doubtless had power to affect humans. Modern astronomy can admit no such things. The planets are lumps of rock at immense distances. How can they affect character?

The answer perhaps is that they do not. It will be recalled that in lamaistic belief, a child born in the usual way can be a *tulku*, a more stable kind of *tulpa* expressing the thoughts and wills of others. In the turbulent 1920s, Mongols hoped to create a national leader in this manner by thinking about him and longing for him. Suppose then that a child is born with tendencies matching the altitude of a planet. Mars is rising, and the child (as will appear in a few years' time) is a born athlete. Could it be that the crucial factor is not the planet's position in itself, but astrologers' knowledge of that position? When many astrologers are thinking about Mars rising with such-and-such a presumed influence, a child born at that juncture might tend, on Tibetan assumptions, to be a *tulku* with a bias expressing the astrologers' thoughts. There is no need to imagine them consciously willing the birth of such a child. Thought-form production can, we are assured, take place inadvertently, simply because people's minds create the conditions for it. On this showing, while there is no causal link between planets and personality, natal astrology is given a semblance of truth through *tulkus* formed because of astrologers' belief in it.

To revert, now, to the miraculous as commonly understood. While few Christian miracles are like lamaistic feats in content, we do have a convergence at the level of ideas. 'Miracle' is a Christian way of denoting something which Lamaistic Buddhism also provides for, though viewing it differently. Phenomena occur which transcend the normal course of nature, and are due to Mind which itself transcends nature. In this context Christians think of the Mind as God, and as causing events which are radically exceptional and properly called miraculous. Lamas are unwilling to speak of miracles, because they do not allow that the exceptions really are so. Just as there is law and logic in the visible world, there is a higher law and logic in the Beyond. Moreover, the lamas continue, this can be learned to some extent. By mental exercises and attunement, an adept can cause extraordinary manifestations of Mind in ways which he intends himself. Thought-forms are the outstanding instance. An advanced being, such as the Bodhisattva spoken of to Mme David-Neel, can inject them into the normal world like an artist adding to a picture. On the face of it this is at odds with Christianity, because, for Christians, the only Mind which can cause such manifestations is God, and he is separate from human minds and outside their control.

However, at least two points imply a blurring of boundaries. First, on the Christian side, we have an instance in tradition, if not in official doctrine, of one human being who can obtain miracles at will, and in effect activate the Beyond so as to produce effects like the Bodhisattva's. This is the Blessed Virgin Mary, whose rapport with God is so perfect that he does whatever she asks. Meanwhile, on the Buddhist side, we have the lamas' admission that thought-forms are more than projections of the adept's ego. Outside factors are present in them. They can appear uncalled-for. They can embody the thoughts of several people rather than one, with the implication of something else at work to blend and harmonise. They can develop a character of their own, and resist dissolution, like Mme David-Neel's monk. They can go off by themselves and act independently. They can oppose or even attack the originator. They can outlive him. In the Shambhala mythos, important thought-forms are said to emanate from a Shambhala which is heavenly as well as earthly, and exists in the Beyond as well as here, with superhuman inhabitants. In fact, while the Beyond may indeed have a logic of its own, it is *other*, active, and not fully comprehensible or controllable.

Lamas' denial of the miraculous is thus hardly more than a quibble over words. But their theory carries us beyond Christianity. It hints that while miracles of the full-blown type are rare, there may be wider classes of happenings in which the Beyond plays a special part: happenings which are more various and more frequent, less plainly supernatural, but still miraculous after their fashion, in the sense that natural causes alone cannot account for them. This would be true, for example, of *tulku* births. But the possibility could extend very much further.

8

Intimations

With these ideas in mind we are justified in moving outside religion again, and turning back at last to an ill-defined realm which has received flattering attention in recent years: the realm of the occult and paranormal – of neo-magic, of extra-sensory perception, of psycho-kinesis.

Exponents of these topics will rise in protest at such a proposition. They will fling back the same denial as Mme David-Neel's lamas. They will insist that the feats which they believe in have no place here, being not mir-aculous but due to little-known human powers, or to forces or agencies which, however obscure, can be studied systematically. Aleister Crowley, the most no-torious of modern magicians, presented 'magick' (his preferred spelling) as a technique for producing willed results, like the secret arts of Pharaoh's wizards in their contest with Moses. This, to him, was the vital point. Details of magical doctrine were secondary. As he put it in a famous passage introducing a manual:

> In this book it is written of the Sephiroth and the Paths, of Spirits and Conjurations; of Gods, Spheres, Planes, and many other things which may or may not exist.
>
> It is immaterial whether they exist or not. *By doing certain things certain results follow*; students are most earnestly warned against attributing objective reality or philosophic validity to any of them.

Here Crowley's statement of the matter is quasi-scientific and wholly anti-miraculous.

But is it correct? Even if we accept magicians' claims about the phenomena that happen, do we find (where they can be pinned down at all) that they happen like this, in a humanly controlled sequence of cause and effect? By the same token, does ESP, so patiently tested by Professor Rhine and his associates, show the regularity which their method of treating it and discussing it would seem to imply? There is a case for regarding such things as real. Is there a case, though, for their having that kind of reality? Despite all the interest which these matters have been arousing since the late 1960s, it remains far from clear what exactly the interest is *in*. The subject is bedevilled by unproved assumptions, question-begging and argument-rigging, not only on the side of believers, but on the side of their professedly rational critics; and more so with the latter than with the former.

A few years ago I aired this theme in a piece of fiction entitled *The Finger and the Moon*. Some of the comments made by reviewers were curiously revealing. Here is a sentence from a notice in the *New Statesman*, that organ of the rational Left:

> This is certainly the most interesting question posed by the novel: why are the notions and attitudes embodied in the word magic gaining ground, particularly among the young?

And here is a sentence from a notice in the *Economist*, that organ of the rational Right:

> This, of course, is the important issue raised by this otherwise unimportant book: why is there a revival of magic, witchcraft, druidism, satanism, all the irrational luggage of organised superstition that western man has been shrugging off these 300 years past?

The same question has been asked, angrily or plaintively, by critics of other books than mine. One might be excused for wondering whether they have ever, truly, wanted an answer. In my own case it was clear that even if the question was posed sincerely, the writers' notions of what would have counted as an answer were straitjacketed by presuppositions. Because, although they complained that the novel failed to offer one, the fact was that it did, and near the beginning where (surely?) no reviewer could have missed it.

I put it in a lecture by a character in the story, an imagined psychologist, and the lecture was based in part on the work of a real and very distinguished one, Viktor Frankl.

'More and more of our patients complain of a sense of meaninglessness in life. More and more often, the reason is the outlook of science. Or what has come through to them as the outlook of science. Sometimes it's called reductionism . . .

'Thinking people tend to feel that science has cut Man down. It's explained away everything that matters in terms of smaller, meaner things that don't matter. Religion is *nothing but* wish-fulfilling fairy-tales. Love is *nothing but* body chemistry. Art is *nothing but* a surge of conditioned reflexes . . .

'Science leaves Man shut-in, futile, doomed. . . . It feeds on the work of its countless laboratories, to trap people in closed systems – chemical, or biological, or physical systems – where all colour has gone and all hope is lost.'

Obviously a reader might comment that while the rebirth of magic and so forth may be an understandable response to this feeling, it is mere escapism, a flight from reason. So I introduced questioners making that very point, and gave my lecturer a counter-attacking reply.

'You claim to speak for scientific, progressive humanism, and you equate it with reason. I'm telling you it hasn't worked. It's supposed to instil devotion to the good of mankind. But apart from a high-calibre few, it doesn't. On the one hand we live in dread of technological horrors. . . . On the other hand there's a powerlessness to do much about it. A failure of will – because of this feeling that a darkness of soul is closing in and death is the end and science has made everything hollow and pointless. Now if that's so (and I can give you evidence, clinical scientific evidence, that it is), then I wouldn't call it a flight from reason to look elsewhere for rescue. It's thoroughly rational. At least, it can be."

What I wanted to convey was that under these mental pressures many people have become seekers after transcendence, not rejecting science within its proper sphere, but reaching out in dissatisfaction to something beyond. Right or wrong, that still seems to me a per-

158

fectly serious answer to the question the book-reviewers posed. But it was not the sort they could admit, or even recognise when they saw it. The trouble was that it dared to suggest a degree of rationality in the seekers' conduct. They were portrayed as in thoughtful pursuit of something which was at least conceivably 'there'. The reviewers, true to the dogmas of scientific humanism, had assumed in advance that it wasn't. Therefore my answer was no answer at all, and their mental blockage was so complete that they implied I hadn't given one, when I had given it on the fifth page and reverted to it a number of times throughout the novel.

This trifle of journalistic history is worth recording, because it helps to clarify issues. Given the widespread outlook which those reviewers evince, what would count as an answer to their question? What kind of inquiry could be accepted as leading to it? In essence the inquiry would have to be sociological and question-begging. An unbelieving researcher would interview believers, ask about their interests and motives, and probe their background and mental make-up. He would then draw conclusions, not by considering whether their beliefs were true, but by trying to pinpoint some psychological defect – some neurosis, let us say — which they had in common. This, if found, would be presented as the source of what is assumed in advance to be a delusion . . . because, as all thinking people know without bothering to investigate, ESP and magical phenomena and the rest don't happen.

Such a procedure might not strike one as very objective, or even very rational. It is not a travesty; I have seen precisely this procedure used to explain sightings of unidentified flying objects. (Sometimes, in unguarded moments, upholders of 'rationality' make amazing admissions. Dr A. L. Rowse, in another review of a book on magic (not mine), once remarked – quite casually, with no apparent awareness of what he was saying – that people who think rationally are wrong more often than others, because they fail to understand the majority

159

who don't. But if reason has any meaning or value at all, it is as a method of arriving at truth; of thinking right. If it is a method of not arriving at truth, of being wrong more often, what use is it? Surely such a notion of rationality is in need of an overhaul?) But to appreciate what this style of thinking involves is to get closer to the immediate issue. The claim of rationality in the dogma that 'these things don't happen' is more specific here than it is when applied to miracles, and, on the face of it, more logical. It rests on a certain notion of what the things are supposed to be; and to some extent, occultists and parapsychologists have themselves to blame for their own dismissal. The would-be-scientific excuse for denying such feats – or rather, refusing to discuss them – is that the evidence for them is 'anecdotal', and a thousand anecdotes do not add up to one scientific argument. What matters is that nobody has ever set up a repeatable experiment, and shown the feats being done to order. Nobody has ever performed them in the presence of sceptics, under properly controlled laboratory conditions. That and that alone would be proof. In its absence they may be treated as fictitious, subjective, accidental, or bogus. So when interest is shown in them, the only admissible reason is that there is something wrong with those who show it.

Now of course this is really question-begging again. What the opponent actually does is to define proof in advance so as to make proof impossible, or very unlikely. Thereby he excludes discussion of topics which he prefers not to discuss. It is special pleading, because he would not apply the same standard to other, less unsettling types of behaviour. It may be true that no one has demonstrated telepathy under laboratory conditions. But does the existence of telepathy depend on anyone's being able to? No experimenter could make a couple fall in love under laboratory conditions. No experimenter could get a great symphony composed or a great poem written under laboratory conditions. Not with the reliability demanded, at any rate. Yet couples

160

do fall in love. Great music and poetry exist. And so perhaps telepathy may.

The point, however, is this. The opponent can get away with his special pleading and his false standard because of the notion, unwisely fostered by many believers, that these feats are conscious and purposive; that in Crowley's words, 'by doing certain things certain results follow'; that the secret lies in unknown powers which some humans possess, and can use at will. This is the age-old claim of magic, and if it is insisted upon, the demand for proof under strict conditions is fair. Magicians and ESP sensitives ought to be able to perform to order, however rigid the controls. The lack of proof that they can does not, in reality, refute magic or ESP. It does raise the question whether magic and ESP are as their advocates have asserted.

So-called anecdotal evidence can be produced in plenty. But is it evidence for human powers or techniques acting within the system; or is it evidence for something more akin to the miraculous – for intrusion by a Transcendence that eludes scientific handling entirely? a Transcendence for which a human being may serve as a contact point; with which he may achieve a rapport, so that it comes through for him with unusual frequency; but which no mere circumscribed ego can consciously control, or reliably use?

In their more confiding moods, occultists are apt to be closer to this position than the proud language of magic implies. They would be less open to criticism if they adopted it frankly. Crowley himself, despite the arrogance of his public claims, admitted in moments of candour that the truth was otherwise. 'Magick,' he once wrote, 'eludes consciousness altogether, so that when one is able to do it, one does it without conscious comprehension, very much as one makes a good strike at cricket or billiards.' He warned his disciples not to suppose that magick could be taught directly, as one might teach a person to drive a car. They could listen to the experiences of senior adepts. They could try magical procedures themselves. They could record what they did, and what – if anything – came of it. Then others, in turn, could reflect on the results. But nothing was automatic, or securely under control.

In *The Finger and the Moon* I fictionalised this theme by way of another imagined lecture.

'Sceptics can always make a [magical] technique look foolish. You know the line. They ask six astrologers to cast the same person's horoscope, and get six different readings, none of them convincing. Yet you also know that expert astrologers do succeed. Not every time – there's always that on-and-off quality – but enough . . .

'Our basic fact is neither consistent scoring by any of these techniques, nor consistent non-scoring. Nor is it a hotchpotch of half-results that might be guesswork or might not. No, it's a record of *some* brilliant successes by every method, often in a series by the same person, but always in a strange now-you-see-it-now-you-don't pattern, with a scrap-heap of failures all around.

'Most modern interpreters of magic would agree what the likeliest reason is. *The technique is not the secret.* The spelt-out drill, the conscious acts which a magician performs, don't account for whatever success he has. They focus his mind on the subject, yes. Or perhaps they just keep it occupied. They may do this better, for him, than anything else would, and he may be right to use them. But the real inner process, of character-reading or prediction or whatever, is . . . other. The same is true of minor magical workings to produce effects, like casting a spell. When a spell gets cast it isn't because of any words the magician recites. If he hits his mark and then tells you how it was done, he's probably rationalising. He may even be deceiving himself.'

If the process is real at all, in fact, it is activated from beyond individual consciousness. The magician's technique is largely a ritual to invite whatever it is that does this. To invite it, not to command it, even if he deludes himself into thinking that he does command. The invitation is sometimes accepted, sometimes refused. As far back as the seventeenth century we find a practitioner who glimpsed the truth. John Aubrey, writing of the mathematician William Oughtred, says this:

> He was an astrologer, and very lucky in giving his judgments
> on nativities; he confessed that he was not satisfied how it
> came about that one might foretell by the stars, but so it was
> that it fell out true as he did often by his experience find; he
> did believe that some genius or spirit did help.

We have got magic away from the lab-test argument, on to ground where opponents must employ a different method of attack – one which they employ anyhow, alongside the lab-test, but which now becomes central. The question is whether the magicians' successes do actually occur, and to what extent. Unbelievers, when forced to face 'anecdotal' evidence that they sometimes do, invoke the laws of probability. If an astrologer makes, say, a hundred predictions, he will score occasional hits by chance. If he makes a thousand, a few may be correct in enough detail to look extraordinary. Chance, nevertheless, is the only factor present. Any notion that astrology works, from whatever cause, is due solely to remembering the few successes, and forgetting or soft-pedalling the many failures. Likewise for numerology and all kindred forms of magic. Unbelievers who have no use for these as techniques have no use for influences from Beyond, either; and when deprived of the lab-test argument, they can still apply the probability argument. However, it is much more shaky. Professor Eysenck's study of natal astrology, mentioned in the previous chapter, may appear to have put matters in a new light, but it is too soon to say what its effect will be, and for the moment we must follow the classic line. Does the probability argument work?

Of course it is right in some degree. It may well dispose of more cases than it fails to dispose of. But it can hardly be the whole truth. Perhaps magical successes really are no more frequent than random expectation. Still they are apt not to follow a random pattern. They bunch, they cluster for a time round a particular person, they come spectacularly and go suddenly. The laws of probability may be upheld in a sense, and yet a query persists.

To cite a famous instance, that is the impression

which open-minded readers get from the Prophecies of Nostradamus. Nostradamus, a sixteenth-century French astrologer, published 942 quatrains foretelling future events over a period of four and a half centuries. Most of these are too obscure to make trustworthy sense, one way or the other. A few can be fitted to facts of history and thus counted as fulfilled. The sceptic will say, 'Quite so, exactly what we might expect to happen by chance.' But the good predictions are not so easily dealt with. In the first place, their scatter is peculiar. They all, or nearly all, concern France or England. Subject to a few doubtful interpretations, Nostradamus never scores a hit with prophecy about any other country, and it is not for want of trying. In the second place, a very few are not just right but astoundingly right, on points of detail which it is hard to imagine anyone guessing. The mere observation that they are very few is not enough to dispose of them.

Suppose a statistician were told the number of people in a crowd. He might predict that about a hundred of the adult males in it would fall within a height range of five feet six to five feet ten. Measurement might then prove him correct, even exactly correct, the number being just a hundred. But suppose further that fifty of them turned out to be five feet six and a half, and the other fifty turned out to be five feet nine and a half. The laws of probability would have been upheld, yes – yet an additional fact would have come to light defying them altogether, and requiring another explanation. So it tends to be with magic, perhaps not often, but often enough to be significant. The magician does not do it himself. Something (I would suggest) works erratically through him. It may give him success no more often than chance would lead us to expect it, but the success, when it comes, has qualities which chance fails to account for. Something Beyond has intervened in the natural order, and we have what can fairly be described as a mini-miracle.

Before pursuing that idea, I should add that my own

experience leaves me sceptical about even the basic probability argument. At this point I must introduce the first of my modest store of personal case-histories. It is anecdotal, alas, but a case-history in this field could hardly be otherwise. At least the anecdote is first-hand.

Early in December 1975, I invited a Tarot expert to give me a reading for the ensuing four months. The expert was Colin Amery, a poet who now lives in New Zealand. We went through a prescribed ritual of cutting the Tarot pack and dealing out cards. He told me that I had a plan for a long and important journey. In January there would be much doubt overhanging it. This would be resolved, and in March it would take place. A woman born under a Fire sign of the Zodiac would be concerned in it. Meanwhile, in January, a new archaeological project would have been brought to my attention, connected with a hill. Towards the end of the four-month period I would probably be moving into a fresh sphere of work and interest.

These were his main forecasts, and they were all fulfilled. The intended journey was to America. Factors beyond my control made it look uncertain in January, but I went in March. The chief purpose was to lecture at a university, under the sponsorship of a woman professor whose birthday was in July under Leo, one of the three Fire signs. The archaeological project was also delivered. A letter came in January from someone who had been trying to organise an excavation at a hill-fort which I had drawn attention to. The letter followed months of silence during which I had almost forgotten the scheme. It informed me, for the first time, that the dig was going ahead. As for the fresh sphere of work and interest, this could be fairly related to a book of mine which, in April, was on the verge of being published and had many consequences.

Colin could have picked up hints for some of this from conversation, but not for all of it. I had not, for example, told him the professor's birthday; I had not even mentioned her. Nor had I spoken of the excavation

165

proposal. In fact I failed to recall it myself during the reading, and throughout December. It only came back to me when the letter arrived.

The sceptic will say: 'Ah, but no doubt you've had your fortune told many times. You're just picking on the one time when it turned out well.' Not so. I have not had my fortune told many times. To the best of my recollection, Colin's Tarot reading was the only fortune-telling I have ever submitted to at the hands of a self-styled expert. It was a unique case, and it worked.

However, it did not dispose me to value the technique as such. I do not believe that the cards foretold anything, or even, strictly speaking, that Colin did. The cards gave him talking points and were doubtless well adapted to that purpose. His dealing and interpreting constituted a kind of patter suited to himself, which helped whatever-it-was-that-knew-what-was-shaping-up to slip in below the threshold of consciousness and cause events in his brain.

Does the same apply to things reckoned as paranormal rather than magical? What about yogic feats, healing, dowsing, extra-sensory perception, metal-bending? Who or what is the actual doer?

There is no single answer. 'Powers' of a sort, more or less under the owner's control, may indeed account for some of them. Perhaps, though, these are not so very mysterious. The scope of psychosomatic action, and of suggestion hypnotic and otherwise, is still imperfectly known. As noted, yogis have demonstrated breath-control and heart-control in the laboratory. Some healers have an impressive record. In such cases there is nothing even quasi-miraculous ... but there need not be anything paranormal either. Scientists may be equal to the challenge, or become so in the near future.

Dowsing is more of a puzzle. In the restricted sense of water-divining, it has been tested with conflicting results. An experiment set up in 1968 by Professor John Cohen, a psychologist, turned out well enough to make

166

him reconsider his scepticism. He buried five cans of water and several dummy containers. The dowser, Robert Leftwich, found three of the five cans and passed over all the dummies. A similar test by the British Army is reputed to have been negative. Both tests were somewhat artificial, and practical field experience is in the dowsers' favour. The difficulty is to explain what happens, and why. It is not due to any mystic virtue in hazel twigs or other devices. When a dowser is near whatever he is concentrating upon, the object he holds is liable to twist, dip or otherwise perform, uncontrollably, whether it is a twig or a plastic strip or a pendulum or a rod pivoted on a handle. While the instrument has no special quality, the person seemingly has, since not everyone can dowse: a minority only, its size being disputed.

The natural explanation (so far as any exists) is subconscious knowledge. A diviner searching for water, an engineer searching for an underground pipe, has a subtle awareness of what the ground surface should look like where a spring is present or a pipe runs below. His knowledge passes unconsciously to his fingers in minimal muscular reactions, and the twig or rod magnifies these.

It may be so. Probably it often is. Yet a doubt lingers as to whether that is the whole story. Here too I can offer a personal history. I have tried dowsing just twice myself, on an archaeological site. Again there is no question of picking out a few special cases from numerous attempts. These two were the only ones in my life. Both were successful, but in very different ways.

The first time, I carried a rod over the grass of an unexcavated part of the site, looking for a trench in the hidden bedrock below, part of the foundation of a hypothetical building. Roughly at a place where this might plausibly have been, the rod twisted in my hand. It did so every time I tried. Digging showed that a trench did indeed pass that point. Subconscious expectation, based on a mental survey, might have accounted for my

167

success. But the second attempt was otherwise, and more striking. I was endeavouring to do the same in a different area – locate a foundation trench in the bedrock, under a stretch of grass where nobody had yet dug. This time the vanished building was not hypothetical. Part of its foundation had already been unearthed in the neighbourhood. Expert opinion and my own judgment combined to insist that another part had to be somewhere under the grass. I paced over the ground again and again. This time the rod failed to twist, at any rate convincingly. At last I gave up. Later, excavation revealed that the plan of the building had been wrongly reconstructed. No foundation trench was there after all. In other words it was as if the rod had known better than I did, and better than skilled archaeologists. Expectation had said the trench must be there. The rod had defied expectation, and been proved right.

How did it know – especially as the power, if any, is acknowledged not to be in the instrument? Its contrasting behaviour the first time and the second could have been accidental, but I went over the ground so often that I think this unlikely. It could have been due to some radar-like faculty in myself, working through the rod – the second time, in defiance of my conscious mind. If neither, it could have been caused by an outside entity with superior knowledge, aware of what was under the topsoil as no living human was . . . in which case, as with successful magic, the events were more akin to the miraculous than to the paranormal. Anyhow it is clear to me that the truth about dowsing is highly unclear. To call it a power or a gift is to play with words. No one know how it works, if it does. No one knows what it is, if it is anything. One certainty (here again) is that it is not a technique that can be used predictably in all contexts, like boiling a kettle. Dowsing is not consciously done, it happens. For a good practitioner, it happens right more often than it does for a poor one, but it does not happen consistently for anybody. Again one scents the possible erratic intrusion.

168

If we turn to the so-called paranormal itself – to ESP, psychokinesis and the rest – the impression is much the same, only more so. The senior experimenter in this field is Professor J. B. Rhine of Duke University, North Carolina. Russian scientists have shown more interest than western ones. However, scientists can be found in all parts of the world who are willing to admit the phenomena. That is proper and reasonable. Whether there is much point in the experiments pioneered by Rhine is another question. The classic type of ESP test consists in an experimenter dealing out a pack of cards with various geometrical shapes on them, while the ESP subject tries to 'sense' which shape is on each card as it comes, there being five possibilities. The assumption in this and all kindred tests is that if a subject keeps scoring better than he would by pure guesswork, he has extra-sensory powers, and something of a scientific nature has been proved about them.

Several difficulties arise. The first is the same that arises with controlled tests of dowsing – that the test is artificial. Finding cans of water, carefully planted to confuse, is not what a dowser in practice does. If there are people who can sense objects at a distance without seeing them, it is certain that in any real-life situation where they actually do it, the objects are not cards with abstract designs on them being turned over in a lab. This criticism is no quibble. Early in the history of experimental psychology, attempts were made to study memory by telling subjects to memorise nonsense syllables. The idea was that in the absence of meaning, everyone was on the same footing and the results were objectively comparable. They were, but they were also trivial. Research made little progress till Professor F. C. Bartlett diverted it on to fresh paths by pointing out that memorising nonsense syllables is not a thing which people normally do. The tests had no relevance to real human behaviour. So also with contrived ESP tests. They are easy to quantify and compare. After their fashion, they are objective. But if ESP happens at all, as a factor in ordinary life, it may not be much like that.

Still, let us assume that such a test has been positive, that a subject has scored consistently well through a series of attempts. Even then the experimenters have no notion how he did it. 'Extra-sensory perception' is simply a phrase. No convincing theory explains what the power is or in what medium it works. No known process can account for an image detaching itself from a card and floating through space into a brain. Hence, no amount of would-be-scientific testing can do more than show that some people can score much better than average. The power, if any, remains obscure. The fact of sustained high scoring, if it is a fact, still does not bring ESP within the domain of science, because there is nothing in science to hitch it on to. As Arthur Koestler remarks, scientific concepts (especially in physics) have become so weird and complex themselves that they no longer supply any basis for denial; but they are of no help in affirmation, they do not relate.

The only useful question is whether the fact itself is real or illusory. The answer is much the same as with magic, neither a straight 'yes' nor a straight 'no'. Some ESP subjects have done amazingly well, and have seemed able to keep it up for a while, or to do well in enough tests in a series to make their average very high. Some have done well in strange, unexpected ways – for example, by repeatedly sensing the card before or after the one being dealt. Scores have been recorded with so great a correct percentage that the odds against pure chance are colossal. With the standard card experiment, a subject tested by Professor Bernard Reiss of Hunter College, New York, was put through 74 deals of 25 cards each and got an average of 18·24 correct guesses per deal – random expectation being 5. Theoretically the dealer would have had to go on for aeons to produce any likelihood of such a sequence. In a test by Helmut Schmidt, the subjects were faced with four lamps that lit up in random order, and had to guess which lamp would light next. The method of randomisation was completely impersonal. In a total of about eighty thousand attempts, the proportion of correct guesses was such that the odds were calculated at ten thousand million to one against.

But no ESP subject has ever done it reliably, at least in circumstances where we can trust the truth of the report. Outstanding scores, when they occur, may be so far above random expectation as to make the idea of an unknown factor seem irresistible. However, they cease, or they come and go and come again with no visible pattern. As my fictitious lecturer said, speaking of magic, the datum is neither consistent scoring nor consistent non-scoring. It is a record of a certain number of brilliant successes, often in a series by the same person, with a scrap-heap of failures all around. The successes may be too brilliant to shrug off, but the failures are never eliminated. Which is also true of more complex activities like telepathy. Telepathy appears to happen, but seldom so as to suggest any faculty that can be defined or scrutinised.

Honestly faced, in fact, much of the alleged paranormal resembles the alleged magical. It looks like a species of the miraculous – a small, unspectacular, but widely encountered species. The human organism has no secret powers of the sort imagined. But it may act as a channel for Something Beyond which can break into the natural order and cause exceptional events, such as brain action corresponding to the designs on unseen cards. These events are irregular. They are not subject to control or prediction. If they have a logic, it is in the Beyond. To study them quasi-scientifically is a proceeding with limited value. It can show that they occur, and, despite wishful thinking and some detected frauds, it apparently has. That is important, but that is all.

Psychokinesis or PK, the ability to move objects without touching them, is usually counted as another branch of the paranormal. There are people, it is claimed, who

171

can mentally influence the fall of dice, so as to make a throw of (say) six occur more often than it should. For those who look for causation – paranormal or otherwise – within the natural order, this presents an even worse problem than ESP. Mental events may have subtle rules of their own, objects like dice must surely obey the gross rules of mechanics.

PK is still too obscure to discuss with any assurance. It may belong with ESP as another version of the mini-miraculous (if we settle on that as the explanation, and succeed in giving it an intelligible meaning). On the other hand it may indeed be a 'power' in the human organism. Russian scientists claim to have discovered at least two psychokinetic adepts, Nelya Kulagina and Alla Vinogradova, who can cause small objects to roll or slide on flat level surfaces, more or less at will.

But if PK is a power, it may not be paranormal. It may be like the better-established yogic powers. Here the much-publicised exploits of Uri Geller have a double interest. Besides doing what purported to be tele-pathy on TV, Geller convinced Professor John Taylor of King's College, London, that he could make objects change shape and fly about without contact; or some-times, with contact but without pressure. Though Taylor accepted that the Geller Effect was real, he denied that it was paranormal, in the sense of eluding materialistic science. When spoons bent and rods leaped across a laboratory, his thoughts turned towards an un-known form of electromagnetism emitted by the brain. That view was presently supported by studies of chil-dren who could do tricks of the same type, bending metal and swinging compass-needles.

Geller himself maintained that his feats defied such physical explanations. Yet he did not claim to have strange powers of his own. He professed to be in touch with higher beings in other worlds, who worked through him. This was his science-fiction version of Something Beyond. Whether he was genuine, self-deceived or a clever hoaxer (a question which the exposures of him do not entirely resolve), he did show signs of grasping what the reality of the so-called paranormal would be like.

To suggest that mini-miracles may happen quite often, and that ESP and telepathy are intrusions from Beyond into the brain's habitual routine, is to invite the retort that the idea of miracles must not be trivialised. From a western point of view a miracle is an act of God, or, at any rate, of a deity. It is a sign with meaning, not a mere trick. And at least in the Christian scheme, it has a spiritual dimension and is linked with holiness. We should not picture God, or any higher being, contriving correct guesses at patterns on cards by persons of no unusual virtue, with no moral or message to be inferred. It is not that such beings are necessarily concerned only with big things – God's eye is on the sparrow – but that it seems unworthy to imagine them causing exceptions in the system where the case is petty and pointless.

A partial answer is that the best attested of modern Christian miracles is the solar movement at Fatima. This, it is worth stressing again, was not only witnessed by a huge crowd (a fact which might be rationalised), but witnessed at virtually the time predicted (a fact which cannot). While it was not trivial like the card-guessing, it has, up till now, presented great difficulties in other respects. The visions and promises leading up to it plainly imply a meaning, but no one discussing it, not the most devout or erudite Catholic, has satisfac-torily explained what the meaning was. As for the spiritual dimension, the sun's antics were seen by believ-ers and atheists, good characters and bad. The anti-clerical editor was one of those who saw it most clearly, and though he confessed it, he was not converted. While Fatima may be unriddled sooner or later, its present opacity is a warning against undue confidence as to what God, or any higher being, would or would not do; or, in the lamas' terms, as to what effects transcendent Mind might or might not produce. Who knows? A swarm of puny but baffling ESP performances might be ordained, collectively, to restrain us from total surrender to the dogmatism of scientists. Trivial in themselves, they might, together, compose a continuing 'sign' of deep import, as a mass of dots composes a newspaper photograph. The suggestion is not frivolous. It is a matter of record that ESP data have had precisely that effect on a number of eminent, scientifically-trained, influential figures: Arthur Koestler, for instance.

Koestler himself, though eschewing gods, is aware that the question of meaning is inescapable. He connects the so-called paranormal with what is sometimes described as synchronicity. The word was coined by the psychologist C. G. Jung in collaboration with the physicist Wolfgang Pauli. It is applied to coincidences which are so far-fetched and so significant that the chance course of events fails to account for them satisfactorily. The relationship between the things or people concerned is supposed somehow to twist the chain of cause and effect, bringing them together when normal causation would have been most unlikely to do so. Some factor is present transcending the laws of probability, as so often in ESP tests.

This can happen at various levels of significance. There are coincidences which seem beyond accident yet have no obvious point. Koestler quotes one from the notebooks of the Austrian biologist Paul Kammerer. His wife, reading a magazine in a doctor's waiting-room, was impressed by some reproductions of paintings by an artist named Schwalbach, and made a mental note of his name with a view to seeing the originals. At that moment the door opened, and the receptionist called out to the patients: 'Is Frau Schwalbach here? She is wanted on the telephone.'

Then there are coincidences which do seem to have a point, but it is not clear what it is. Jung himself tells a famous anecdote:

> A young woman I was treating had, at a critical moment, a dream in which she was given a golden scarab. While she was telling me this dream I sat with my back to the closed

window. Suddenly I heard a noise behind me, like a gentle tapping. I turned round and saw a flying insect knocking against the window-pane from outside. I opened the window and caught the creature in the air as it flew in. It was the nearest analogy to a golden scarab that one finds in our latitudes, a scarabaeid beetle, the common rose-chafer (*Cetonia aurata*), which contrary to its usual habits had evidently felt an urge to get into a dark room at this particular moment.

Whether or not the beetle's arrival actually had a point, Jung, with some presence of mind, speedily gave it one. The patient had been blocking the treatment by her rigidly rationalistic point of view. He handed her the beetle, saying 'Here is your scarab', and she was so shaken that her resistance crumbled.

At this level we might bring in much of the telepathic and ESP data. Two people have the same thought at the same time. Or an image in the brain coincides with the image on a card. Arguably, neither event causes the other, and the whole fuss over the 'power' involved is a mare's nest. Somehow the affinity itself is the root of the coincidence, and the cause, if that is an appropriate term, is outside the system.

Farther up the scale is serendipity, the knack which some people possess of discovering useful things or important facts when they are not looking for them. The discovery pursues the person rather than the other way round. Farther up again are happenings which religious minds regard as special providences, acts of divine guidance, answers to prayer, or, indeed, miracles; such as a wildly unlikely 'chance' meeting with the one person on earth who can help in a crisis. Here the sense of an overriding knowledge and purpose may be overwhelming.

If we think of intervention by Something Beyond in this context, certain notions begin to take shape. Whatever the Something is, it produces events which have an air of significance. The exceptions which it injects into the system to produce such results may, in themselves, be very small. With the non-chance happenings just considered, it is enough to imagine irregularities so minute

175

as to be undetectable. Tiny 'synchronicities' are slipped into the brain which result in telepathy and ESP; or in states of mind, inspirations, decisions, which would not have occurred otherwise. Everything that follows, however sweeping, is due to normal cause-and-effect set off by the minimal brain-event. The constant tendency in these mini-miracles is to contrive a relationship or correspondence, a happening that is intelligible rather than random, and makes sense. An image in the brain matches the image on a card, and the ESP subject records a positive score. Or an impoverished inventor, and a millionaire able to finance him, have a whim to sit on the same park bench at the same time.

As remarked, the phenomena vary over a wide range of size and significance. Thus far we might suppose that this variation lies in the consequences only, and that the actual miracles which set them in motion are all 'mini'. But there is no logical need for that restriction. If we once concede miracles at all, we can allow that they vary in size themselves. By so doing we can extend the concept to cover miracles in general, the traditional kind as well as these. If the Something Beyond can produce exceptional events below the threshold of human perception, perhaps it can produce them above it as well, whether or not they actually are perceived.

Some that are, possibly, are the thought-form phenomena known to Tibetan mystics. Less exotic are miraculous cures, as reputed at Lourdes, where the state of the patient's body before and after can be seen. Other such maxi-miracles are the levitations ascribed to saints, such as Joseph of Cupertino. According to Christian teaching these are significant as the small ones are – more so – though, as a rule, in some other way than by synchronicity.

We have not parted company with the Christian view. The Something Beyond that works exceptions in the system can, if desired, be identified with God. If we prefer not to connect God with a swarm of mini-miracles that appear petty, we may picture him delegating powers to intermediate beings who are also Beyond, such as angels or spirits. The Gospel miracles remain in a class by themselves if we wish it so, because Christ alone among men was God and united the two realms. He alone could work miracles at will, and not merely invite them.

Indeed, an awkwardness in Christian thinking can now be removed. Special providences, and answers to prayer, have always been a perplexity. Most of them are asserted by theologians to be non-miraculous. They happen, it is explained, in the normal course of events, but only because God has somehow affected this. The problem is to see how he can do so without going the whole way, without injecting an exception into the system – in other words, working a miracle. Even if he does no more than prompt X to go out for a walk during which he will meet Y, something has to happen in X's brain which would not have happened without God's action, and therefore has no natural cause. It is an exception to the brain's normal functioning: a miracle, however minute, leading to a consequence which is properly 'wondered' at. There seems to be no way of picturing divine intervention without making it frankly miraculous. Yet that is how theologians do want to picture it.

One may doubt whether they have ever succeeded. Their answers are abstruse. As we have seen (pages 44–5), they depend on arguments about the nature of time and how God stands outside it. Such contortions may be logical, but they are now beginning to look superfluous. The suggestion is that miracles in the large-scale sense – the kind which Christians are rightly reluctant to spread around too lavishly – are not the only ones. There is a far greater class of irruptions from Beyond, mini-miracles, which need not be distinguished from them; and most divine interventions can be provided for thus, painlessly, because they can be confined to events in the brain. This is often the case even when it appears not to be. Jung's beetle hit the window when his patient was telling him her dream. But perhaps she was moved to tell her dream at the moment when the beetle was approaching the window. The sea was calm when the British army needed to escape from Dunkirk. But perhaps, in answer to prayer, its commanders were moved to fall back on Dunkirk at a time when the sea there would be calm.

The Christian stress on meaning is certainly sound, and compels us to face the essential issue. 'Synchronicity', of course, is only a word, explaining nothing. Jung tried to connect it with the Unconscious, a manoeuvre which was of little help. It is hard to make any sense of it without postulating something of a mental nature behind the events, and something more active and specific than any Unconscious, whether or not we call it God. Rather than admit this, the sceptic will dismiss synchronicity altogether with the same argument deployed against fortune-telling. 'Granted that you and your old friend Hector, whom you hadn't seen for years, did check in at the same hotel in Hong Kong on the same evening. Granted that neither of you had been in Hong Kong before. Granted, even, that when you had dinner together he gave you some advice which altered your whole life. But you meet hundreds of people in hundreds of places. It isn't surprising that one meeting out of the hundreds should chance to be special and significant. You notice it and remember it, that's all.'

The only way I can see to deal with this comment – and, in the process, to infer more precisely what the unseen agency or agencies may be like – is to pile up anecdotal evidence. The sceptic may object, but it will have become plain that anecdotal evidence is the only evidence there is ever likely to be, one way or the other; just as it is the only evidence for what goes on when somebody writes a poem . . . and after all, poems do get written. Here I must revert once more to my own experience. That is the source for the only anecdotes which I feel sure enough about, not as being spectacular proofs,

178

but as being case-histories where all the vital facts are in my possession.

Four incidents in my life strike me as having outstanding interest from this point of view. I could add others, but these four are conspicuous. They are not trivial. All were associated with major decisions, which had crucial and lasting effects. If I number them in order of time, No. 1 happened in August 1947, No. 2 in May 1955, No. 3 in December 1964, and No. 4 in January 1974. They were linked in pairs, No. 1 with No. 3 and No. 2 with No. 4. However, if they are taken in the order in which they happened, the story is more straightforward and the logic, or apparent logic, is clearer.

1. The summer of 1947 was a period of intense pressure, distress and indecision. Among other factors I had been taking an interest in matters Indian, both ancient and modern (that was the summer of Indian independence), and it seemed to me that there was an important potentiality there, but its nature failed to emerge. When I discussed my interest with a Jesuit at Farm Street in London, he urged me to visit a priest of the same order, Father Weaver, who was stationed in India but was then temporarily in England owing to illness. I had never heard of him before, but went to see him in hospital. We had a talk which was frankly unenlightening. Shortly after, however, in what appeared to be an answer to certain prayers for guidance, the mental message came simultaneously to my wife and myself: 'Go and join Father Weaver in India.'

At the time, this was of no evident use whatever. There was no serious question of actually going, and no reason to think that Father Weaver would want me or could do anything for me. Our meeting in fact had been rather uncongenial. He was seldom in England, and seemed to have been brought into my vicinity and thrust at me by his Farm Street colleague as answering my need. Yet that was all. I never had any further contact

179

with him. Nothing remained to me but a puzzled belief that India should be kept in mind. For reasons which I will not go into, this was just enough to help with my immediate problems, but no more. The significance of the message did not appear till seventeen years later, as a result of case No. 3.

2. My serious career as a writer, and, indeed, the whole style of my effective life, originated in 1955 when I became involved with Glastonbury – with its mythology (Arthurian and otherwise), with the trains of thought which the mythology opened up, and with the sense of an abiding mystery destined to unfold again. I had taken a vague interest in the legends before, and been impressed more sharply when passing through the place in a bus, but had never set foot there. In May 1955 I was in Canada. Glastonbury was remote and unthought-of.

As in 1947, a crisis of doubt and indecision exerted pressure. I was then working in Toronto. Something, I have no recollection what, recalled Glastonbury to mind. I went to Toronto Public Library to see what it had on the subject. It turned out to have several books, including one or two which were surprisingly obscure for a library so far from the spot. Among the collection was Christopher Hollis's first book, *Glastonbury and England*. I knew of Christopher Hollis and, in fact, had sometimes had an odd feeling that he was going to figure in my life. (I do not expect anybody to attach importance to my memory of a 'feeling'; but astrologers may relish the fact that he and I share the same birthday, March 29th.) While knowing of Hollis, I do not think I had ever heard of this book. Reading it, I found that it mentioned a prophecy attributed to the last of the Glastonbury monks, Austin Ringwode, that the ruined Abbey's desolation would not last for ever. 'The Abbey will one day be repaired and rebuilt for the like worship which has ceased; and then peace and plenty will for a long time abound.'

The words hit me with the force of a revelation, not

180

because I have any faith in such prophecies, but because they were apt to me personally. They gave me my orders. Glastonbury was going to be reborn and that was what I had to work for. Since writing was my only talent, the first step for me to take was to write a book about Glastonbury. I returned to England, visited the place, and sold the idea of the book to Collins, its original publishers. It appeared in 1957 as *King Arthur's Avalon*, and has sold continuously and in large numbers ever since. At that juncture it was impracticable to go and live in Glastonbury, but I was convinced that I would sooner or later. Meanwhile visits to the place continued, and the paths I was discovering stretched on and on, into Arthurian and other fields with more books resulting.

After research and reflection and a lapse of time, the message of the prophecy did not survive in its pristine form. I remained convinced that I would settle in Glastonbury myself and that some sort of renewal would take place there, but recognised that the rebirth of the Abbey was a dubious proposition to say the least, not to be insisted on literally or exclusively. It was enough, by then, that the main point had been made and I was committed. In view of various results which have followed, I have never had a moment's doubt that the commitment was right.

But I did learn a remarkable fact about the message itself. As I read book after bok, exploring Glastonbury's history and legends, I never came across any further allusion to Austin Ringwode or his prophecy. Finally I asked Christopher Hollis where he had got the story. He was no longer sure, but referred me to an old guidebook which he thought quoted it. I found that it did not. Another historian told me that the prophecy could be traced to a nineteenth-century magazine article, but no further, and that Austin Ringwode was a suspect character anyhow, because there was no record of a monk at the Abbey with that name. In other words the trigger which set me off, determining (and rightly determining) my whole life, was quite probably a mere piece of romantic fiction and an almost forgotten one. Certainly it has never figured in accepted local tradition. In 1955, so far as I know, it was preserved in only one book, Christopher Hollis's. Even this was out of print and extremely rare; I have never seen it anywhere else, except in the British Museum. Yet Toronto Public Library had that copy; and when I was in acknowledged need of guidance and purpose, and mentally ready for it, I was in Toronto and went to the library and found it.

3. In December 1964 a phase of purposive work seemed to have ended in the doldrums. The publishers of *King Arthur's Avalon* and my next three books had turned down two further suggestions. I did not feel that the themes I had already handled could, at that juncture, be pursued any further. Things seemed to be closing in, and after months of doubt I could not see which way to go next.

About Christmas I had a long, complicated dream in which I felt that a hint was struggling to get through, but most obscurely. In one of the most vivid of several scenes, a gravely ill patient was said to require the services of a doctor named Peter Bridge.

The following day, by apparent accident, I met a real physician whom I knew slightly and who had figured in the dream himself. He invited me to his house, where I met his wife. I mentioned the dream and learned, for the first time, that she was a Jungian analyst. She offered some ideas. These were not very lucid, but they set me thinking on fresh lines. I succeeded in interpreting 'Peter Bridge' for myself. A recent news story had been a visit to India by the Pope, occupant of Peter's chair, and Pontiff – a title of Latin origin which goes back to a connection of priests with bridges, *pontes*. The hint was that I might solve my problems and move forward by renewing active attention to India, a country which the Pope, 'Peter Bridge', had placed in the spotlight. A week or two later this notion became specific. It occurred to me to take up a long-standing but dormant interest in Mahatma Gandhi. My work on Gandhi and his mythos of Indian nationalism (published in 1968) proved to be not only a break-out, but a key to new modes of thinking relevant to what I had already done, as appears in a further book, *Camelot and the Vision of Albion.*

The point of course is not that I had the 'Peter Bridge' dream, which any psychologist would be happy to explain without resort to influences from outside. The point is that while it was fresh in memory, I happened to run into my doctor acquaintance who had been in the dream, and whom I probably did not meet more than three or four times a year. Through him moreover I met his wife, who (though I had had no notion of this before) was possibly the one person in that town qualified to give me an interpretation with any value.

The incident had a curious sequel. After working on Gandhi for a while I became aware of two things. One was that he was affectionately known to his followers as Bapu, Father. The other was that when put on trial in 1922 he gave his occupation as 'farmer and weaver'. These facts together at last elucidated the cryptic message in case No. 1. All three elements applied to Gandhi. It was at Farm Street that I had been referred to Father Weaver. 'Join Father Weaver in India' was just the sort of symbolic language which a dream, or subconscious inspiration, might well have tossed up to convey the meaning, 'Interest yourself in Gandhi'. Only . . . Father Weaver was a real person, who had appeared from nowhere at that moment. Furthermore, in 1947 I did not know of Gandhi's 'Bapu' nickname, nor did I know that he had ever called himself a weaver – not, after all, the kind of self-description you would expect from him. If nothing was at work but my own subconscious, that subconscious would have had to contrive a far-fetched coincidence with neither the knowledge nor the ability required to set it up.

4. The conviction that I was meant to live in Glaston-

183

bury, and eventually would, persisted without flagging. In 1971 I moved to Blandford in Dorset, and thereafter visited Glastonbury a little more often, but there was still no sign of my being able to live there. During 1971–2 I wrote *The Finger and the Moon*, located in a fictitious house within sight of Glastonbury Tor which was run as a school of magic and occult philosophy.

A well-known figure in Glastonbury was a Mr J.S. He lived in a house on the lower slope of the Tor. I met him once or twice in the town, but never went to his house and knew nothing about it. In 1973 I heard that he was selling it and moving away. It was reported that he already had a buyer, and it seemed that there would be no point in my making any inquiries, so I made none. Uncertainty continued.

In January 1974 a Dutch television producer came to me in Blandford saying he wanted to make a programme which would include references to the Arthurian legend. I told him that we should go to Glastonbury, and mentioned a teacher whom I knew there as a person who should be interviewed, though it would be difficult to reach him during the day. When the TV crew arrived at my then home, we went to Glastonbury together, and stopped at the foot of the Tor. It was raining so hard that filming was impossible. After a while I got out of the car to look for signs of a break in the weather. Immediately behind the car was the teacher we wanted to find, in conversation with Mr J.S.

I introduced him to the Dutch producer, and, while they were talking, asked J.S. about the sale of his house. He said that after months of negotiations the deal had fallen through, and he had just reduced the price by £3,000. This reduction made it feasible for me to think of buying it myself. I asked if he would consider this, and he agreed. The rain stopped. It had lasted just long enough to produce the meeting. The Dutch TV crew now moved on up the Tor.

A few days later I visited the house for the first time to look over it. He then told me that it had once belonged to Dion Fortune, the novelist and exponent of esoteric matters, and that she had run it as a school of magic and occult philosophy – like my imaginary house in *The Finger and the Moon*, invented without knowledge of it two years before.

It was surely excusable to see the hand of destiny after so many years. The house was obviously the right one for me. To bring about the moment when I offered to buy it, a whole group of factors had had to converge – the failure (at that precise point in time) of the prolonged negotiation over the previous offer; the arrival of the Dutch television team on my doorstep; the rain; the simultaneous presence at the foot of the hill, weather notwithstanding, of J.S. and the teacher.

Since 1974 and my advent in that house, a number of developments, due to my being in it and to its consequent use for various activities, have amply justified the move.

It seems to me that two main considerations arise.

First, the sceptical theory of the 'odd lucky hit' fails to hold water. It might if I had had many crises of indecision, and something extraordinary had happened in cases 1, 2 and 3 and not the rest. It might if over the years I had more or less invited guidance, and multiplied possibilities by my own acts – hanging round libraries seeking omens in books, noting my dreams and trying to interpret them, haunting house-agents and housevendors in Glastonbury, till accident delivered the goods.

But it was not so. The sort of crisis underlying 1, 2 and 3 has been infrequent in my life. I can think of one more, perhaps two, which no extraordinary event came to resolve. Even with both added the fact remains: when such a crisis has occurred, the extraordinary event has happened more often than not. Three out of four, or even five, really cannot count as merely the few lucky hits which are remembered.

As for inviting guidance, it is true I have often

browsed in libraries, but very seldom with that aim in mind. I take little interest in my own dreams, and have few which I recall after waking. I never make any effort to recall them. Those which do linger are mostly trivial. The dream in December 1964 was almost the only one in my life which I have recorded, pondered, and seriously probed in search of a meaning, and the only one I have discussed with a psychologist. It was unique, and it not only worked but produced the psychologist who helped me to see how. On the final point, house-hunting, there was certainly a time when I asked agents in Glastonbury to send me notices of houses for sale, but I never paid much attention to these, and never reached the point of going to view one. By 1974 the sending of notices had ceased, and it would be fair to say that I was not house-hunting in Glastonbury at all, only keeping myself receptive. Let me repeat, I had not raised the question even with J.S. He and his house had to be pushed at me before I took any action, and when this happened it was not simply a house but the most curiously 'right' house which the town could offer.

I find it easier to believe in some kind of intervention from Beyond than to ascribe everything to chance. But the question 'Intervention by whom or what?' raises perplexing issues. Intervention by God? With my four case-histories, there are obstacles in the nature of the events. Granted, three have a religious content – Jesuits, an abbey, the Pope. That, however, need be no more than a reflection of some of my interests at the time. I do not feel that the mini-miracles involved, if they are, quite suggest Supreme Deity.

Here 'Father Weaver' strikes me as crucial. On the one hand, although it looks like a trick of the sub-conscious, it cannot have been entirely that. I could not have contrived Father Weaver's presence, indeed had never heard of him, and also I lacked the data that gave him significance for me. On the other hand this event makes dubious sense as guidance from God. Strictly speaking it was not really guidance at all, but a sort of

186

Catch-22. It drew my attention to Gandhi, but in such a way that I could not know it, could not decipher the message, till I had approached Gandhi by a different route, and studied his career enough to learn about 'Bapu' and the little-known statement of his occupation. I had to be guided to Gandhi in order to discover that I had been guided to Gandhi. God, let me say with due reverence, could arrange a better message than that.

What kind of denizen of the Beyond could be pictured stepping in so peculiarly? Without prejudice to miracles worked by God, I would suggest that many strange events (such as these) look like the work of less exalted beings. Whatever they may be, they transcend material nature but have their own limits. They know more than we do – at least in some respects – and perhaps through delegation they can make exceptions in the course of events, mini-miracles if not the maxi variety. But they need not be gods. I see them as more like the tutelary spirits of pagan lore, or the guardian angels of traditional Christianity. Many have special links with particular individuals or places. Where one of them has an interest in a person, he (or she or it) may be so close to the person as to be virtually a higher self. Such an entity may interpose in the person's life, not only by prompting and helping, but by inducing chance-defying phenomena – ESP, for instance – which give him an appearance of having paranormal powers. He hasn't. It is his unseen companion who has, and the companion may exert them at times but is not to be commanded.

If such beings exist, the exceptions they work in nature are significant, just as God's are held to be. Their miracles, however minor, are more than tricks. But they are not omnipotent or anything like it. Their behaviour may be odd, offbeat, puzzling. They may be unable to get through properly. Or they may judge mystery to be better than clarity, as, perhaps, with Father Weaver. If it is asked how such a vagary as that can be construed as a 'sign' or message, the answer may be that the entity – the guardian angel, or whatever term we use – is not so

187

much saying anything as signalling its own presence, with long-term intentions. 'You won't understand this, for the moment, but it will nag at you; you will at least suspect that there was more in it than chance; and one day, when you do understand, you'll know there was. Let that be a sign and a reminder. The world of appearances is not all. I'm here. You may choose to think of me as your guardian angel or your patron saint or your grandfather's ghost or Lady Luck; it doesn't matter very much, so long as you grasp the main point. And then maybe our relationship can progress and become more fruitful.'

Conclusion

Out of all this, the outlines of what scientists call a 'model' may now emerge.

First we can clear away much nonsense by admitting that within its own sphere, the hard-headed view is right. The natural world does obey scientific laws, at least at the level of our own perceptions, and to say that these laws are statistical rather than rigid is not to blur them. Being statements of 'what usually happens', they cannot pronounce one way or the other on miracles. No rule can preclude exceptions; no law can veto happenings which may fall outside it, inadmissibly-improbable happenings, happenings with no natural cause. But the alleged paranormal – extra-sensory perception, for instance – is another matter. Scientists have every right to question claims about occult powers, and processes said to lie within the natural order but to obey laws not recognised by science. Disbelief may well be justified here. Probably the human organism is very much as biologists and psychologists assert it to be. There is no proof that any persons exist who can perform feats of magic at will, or practise ESP to order, in virtue of secret knowledge or obscure faculties in themselves.

Only . . . we must not halt there. Facts are facts. Apparent magical feats do get performed. Apparent ESP does take place. We can begin to picture such things correctly by transferring their causes to the miraculous side. Meaningful strangenesses are induced in the system far more often than Christian teaching has assumed. But the actual miracles at the root of such events usually happen in the brain, on too tiny a scale to perceive. We see only the results, when the brain-events come through in overt behaviour – apparent magic (successful fortune-telling for instance), apparent ESP. Or inspired decisions, or actions leading to astounding co-incidences. The overt behaviour is not miraculous in itself, but it flows from brain-events which are.

The source of all exceptions in nature, whether small-scale as here or large-scale as in the miracles of religion, is a hierachy of Mind above our limited brains: not physically above, but in the structure of what is some-times called Inner Space. Our brains belong to the natu-ral, scientific order. We have, however, a fitful and fumbling contact with the mind-realm Beyond, which transcends that order. It not only transcends it but can override it. In different degrees at different levels, it has the power to inject exceptions into the system. It does. It is active, not passive, and its interventions make sense, they are not poltergeist whimsies.

Because of its power to overrule nature, the mind-realm may be described as supernatural. However, that is a tricky word. It may also be described as the realm of the divine, because if anything is divine it is there. Again the word should be used with caution. But granted such an extension of meaning, the definition of a miracle as a divinely ordained exception can stand.

Our own concepts of personality cannot really be im-posed on that realm. Closest to human individuals, we may imagine entities who are, in effect, higher selves associated with them – guardian angels more or less, though it need not be inferred that they are con-ventionally angelic. Each one expresses itself in the life of the person allied to it. This is done chiefly through mini-miracles, undetectable brain-events which are magnified into behaviour that would not have occurred otherwise. The overt results often fall under the heading of synchronicity. Meaning is infused into the random flux by the setting up of arresting coincidences. Some-times these come singly as events with a message or warning for the person concerned. Sometimes they take the shape of a series of trivia with cumulative effect, as in a long run of successful ESP trials.

190

Such phenomena may create an illusion of paranormal powers, and they happen more often for some people than for others, owing to a better rapport. The higher self, in fact, is what magicians and ESP sensitives usually invite. They may invite successfully, but they cannot insist. Hence, even the illusion of their having powers of their own is seldom sustained. William Oughtred the astrologer (page 163) grasped the main point three hundred years ago.

The higher self may act in other ways than by synchronicity. There is no reason why it should not be seen, for example, as helping to inspire poetry and music. Certainly it may well prompt such sudden, unexplained intuitions as underlie many major advances in science. Here the remarks of Professor W. H. Thorpe, the distinguished zoologist, come in aptly. Written some years ago, they remain valid.

If we look through the list of recent Nobel prizewinners it becomes obvious that many, perhaps a large majority, achieve this by great leaps of imaginative insight; leaps which, at the time they were made, may have had very little experimental or observational basis. Almost at random one can think of the concept of the double helix ... of quantum mechanics ... of complementarity. All these in their inception were far removed from the work of the laboratory. Yet they played their role as great scientific theories because, though imaginative constructions of wide generality, they were also close enough to physical or biological reality to allow experimental verification.

(*The Times*, January 25th 1969)

Professor Thorpe is pointing towards what many psychologists would call 'the unconscious'. It would be quite proper to suppose that the higher self by whatever name, and the individual it goes with, are not separate beings arbitrarily linked together, but are somehow united, so that 'the unconscious' is really a partial and inadequate image of the higher self. On this showing, man is (so to speak) binary, and has another centre of consciousness in the Inner Space of the so-

191

called unconscious. Jung glanced at that possibility himself, though he quickly rejected it. I put it into *The Finger and the Moon*.

Much the same notion has been expressed by others in a variety of ways. Professor Robert Tocquet, author of *The Magic of Numbers*, has this to say of those strange people known as lightning calculators, who have no outstanding mental abilities yet can do gigantic sums in their heads, sometimes while keeping up a conversation:

> It appears that the mathematical answers obtained by the lightning calculators, or more exactly by those calculators whose output is spontaneous, are the emergence in the domain of conscious ideas of a psychic operation accomplished in the depths of the being and in which the normal consciousness plays sometimes only a very small part.
>
> And this deep region is nothing else but the *daimon* of Socrates, the *theos* of Plotinus, the *planetary genius* of Paracelsus, the *transcendental ego* of Novalis, the *subliminal self* of Myers, the *unknown guest* of Maeterlinck, and, according to the term I have frequently employed, the *subconscious* or the *unconscious* of the psychists. But 'unconscious' not, it would seem, because it lacks consciousness in itself, but only because our normal consciousness does not ordinarily perceive it.
>
> In any case it appears that this cryptic 'I', often unknown to consciousness, is the seat of those more or less mysterious phenomena which range from dreams to precognition, through stages which include artistic, poetical or literary creation, the intuition of genius, the gift of calculation, telepathy and extra-sensory perception.

Since the lightning calculators themselves do seem able to do it to order, at least over longish periods of their lives, it is uncertain how far their feats should be classed with the others. But the drift of Professor Tocquet's remarks is evident.

Past the level of 'higher selves', the mind-realm Beyond must be acknowledged an even profounder mystery. Religions profess to map it out, and they make it the source of the miracles they assert, so far as they assert any: large miracles, visible exceptions in nature, like a terminal cancer suddenly clearing up. In that country we may, if we wish, locate souls of the dead; saints; gods and angels; malignant spirits or devils. Supposedly at the apex of all is – in Jewish or Christian terms – God; in Hindu or Buddhist terms, That which may be apprehended as the One Mind, from which all other minds are derived, and with which they are all in unity, though the unity is veiled by illusion.

The western tradition stresses God's uniqueness and supernatural character. It maintains that miracles (at least in the visible sense) are worked by him and no other being, though prayers at all levels may dispose him to work them, and human beings even in this life, usually saints, can occasion them and focus them. The eastern tradition, as a rule, denies miracles altogether, because it does not draw the same distinctions. It is much more prone to marvels but claims that they are all part of total reality, and obey some sort of cosmic law. However, it locates that law outside the material order, so the difference is not as sharp as it looks. Strictly within nature the marvels *are* exceptions. Their source is Beyond, and while the Beyond may function logically, its logic is its own.

The question really is whose will is at work, and in what spirit. The great thaumaturgists of Hindu legend are close to being magicians, manipulating the Beyond by their own powers, and commanding the gods. Their exceptions in nature are not divinely ordained and, in that sense, the denial that these are miracles is correct. But Lamaistic Buddhism carries the same kind of thinking further, to a position not so very remote from the Christian. It teaches, as we have seen, that adepts can cause – or at any rate, occasion – manifestations of the One Mind which defy normal experience. These are thought-forms: *tulpas* or *tulkus*. Up to a point the adept may seem to be doing it himself. But thought-forms have an autonomy which shows that there is more to them than the activity of the adept's ego. The Beyond is at work in them. They may appear inadvertently. They may

193

acquire a life of their own, turning against the adept, and surviving his death. In the *yidam* version of the exercise, the student attains enlightenment by grasping that what has happened must be seen in terms of self-identification with the One Mind from which all things ordinary and extraordinary proceed.

Here the divergence from Christianity is not so much in the theory as in the attitude. The lama works on thought-formation as a spiritual exercise. He is warned, indeed, against laying too much stress on the phenomena when they come; in themselves they are not the object of what he is doing, however important they may be to his progress; he must think of them as happenings rather than as feats of magic. Nevertheless he may spend a long time in trying to reach the stage where the right attunement is attained and they do happen. His own will is involved. The Christian mystic never attempts such an exercise. If he achieves sanctity, miracles may happen for him. But he knows that they probably will not, and the notion of pursuing sanctity with the wish that they should, even as a step on the road, is a false emphasis likely to defeat itself. His own will is excluded.

There remains, however, one case where Christian and Lamaistic ideas might be held almost to coincide. The Virgin Mary of traditional popular devotion is the perfectly-attuned human being, who can (in effect) produce miracles at will because God always does what she wishes, the Beyond always acts for her. As a wonder-worker she is not easily distinguished from the Bodhisattva described by the Dalai Lama to Alexandra David-Neel – the utterly wise, compassionate being who can act in many places at once, control natural phenomena, make people and buildings and features of the landscape appear and change at need. In a story mentioned in Chapter Four, the apparition of Mary which takes the place of the renegade nun is, in effect, a *tulpa*. Admittedly she is glorified, and in the other world herself. But her status there is only an extension of her status on

194

earth, where she was Mother of God the moment Christ was conceived, and where, as a boy and even afterwards, he was obedient to her. Some legends, such as those fostered by Maria d'Agreda, portray Mary as working miracles during her earthly life.

Legends, yes, but they bring us to a final question that is concerned with realities. Can we cultivate the miraculous? Can we do anything to make irruptions from the Beyond (benign ones, of course) more likely to happen?

In the time-honoured Christian scheme, this is ruled out on moral grounds. Miracles are incidental to holiness, and holiness, not miracles, must be the goal. Also, since God alone works them, any miracle-seeking beyond prayer is impious; it is attempting to harness God. However, perhaps by now our ideas have expanded. Such objections may well apply to the kind of miracles Christian hagiography talks about, but they need not apply generally. If we admit mini-miracles in inspiration and telepathy, we shall find indeed that they are often said to have happened for saints, yet they hardly seem to go with sainthood in any essential way, or to be symptoms of it. Their moral atmosphere may be neutral, and their pursuit for their own sake legitimate. Furthermore, if we allow that they are worked by 'higher selves' however regarded, the blasphemy or absurdity of trying to harness God need not arise. The whole thing is on a humbler level. On that level at least, it is surely harmless to seek attunement and invite miracles, so long as one is free from delusions of achieving magical powers.

Whether it is equally harmless to aspire higher, I am not certain. The lamas' thought-form exercises have been repeated by westerners – not only Mme David-Neel – and they do seem to produce miracles on a visible scale, or at any rate, sustained hallucinations in several people at once, which are quasi-miracles in themselves. Roerich's UFO remains a formidable riddle. Then there is the conjecture that the *tulku* theory might account for that warping of probabilities proved by the Gauquelins, which, on the face of it, supports natal astrology, but may have quite a different meaning. While there is something here, it is most obscure. The wisdom and ethics of plunging deeper in, like the wisdom and ethics of experimental drug-taking, are open to dispute.

Reverting to the safer mini-miraculous, and how it might be fostered, we may recall the theory that telepathy and kindred phenomena were more common in the pre-scientific phase of our ancestry. When the cosmic gods took over, and their more legalistic ideas of order were planted in the minds of their worshippers, interventions from Beyond certainly did come to be seen starkly as exceptions, with stress on their being so. Even the 'mini' variety ceased to be seen unreflectively as all in the day's work. They tended to become self-conscious, abnormal, questionable. The seers and prophets of the Old Testament were rare characters visited by the Holy Spirit, and set apart from other men. That growing sense of restriction is doubtless the reason why such events took to happening less, and why, in the present science-oriented atmosphere, they have become very elusive indeed. Over the centuries, changing mental habits have raised barriers. Today those barriers have risen high. A spurious, sham-scientific common sense closes most people in. It is hard for the Beyond to get through.

That state of affairs is now widely recognised and rightly rebelled against, but usually (as my character in the novel observed) by resorting to such dubious remedies as occultism. The impulse is rational, the attempted solution less so. A wiser course, and one more relevant here, is simply to lower the barriers; to cultivate an acceptance that miracles (mini or otherwise) *can happen*; to invite the higher self or guardian spirit from which, apparently, they are likeliest to come. If enough people come to agree that this is a good and sane thing

196

to do, specific methods of doing it – meditation techniques, for instance – may well develop.

Have we any hint at what such methods might involve? This, perhaps: that somewhere in the depths of the mystery there is a sexual element. It is psychological rather than biological. So far as the history of religion can be deciphered, the great gods of cosmic regularity, who squeezed the exceptional, were male gods. The previous age, when minds were more receptive to the Beyond, was an age when goddesses were powerful – even, in places, paramount. In view of the blending and overlap among them, it has often been construed as the age of 'The Goddess', the one Eternal-Womanly under numerous guises. Whether or not this view is sound anthropologically, it has meaning on the psychological level.

An immediate point illustrating the quality of the Goddess-world is that the intervention from Beyond which we call 'inspiration' has so often been symbolised by a female figure: in Greece the Muse, in some Asian countries a Wisdom-Goddess. The fitness of this idea was so firmly entrenched, so early, that even the triumph of the male failed to cancel it. Apollo took charge of poetry and music in principle, but the Muse herself, divided into nine departmental aspects, was not to be banished. She continued to inspire actual poets and musicians. The eastern Wisdom-Goddess even managed to get a footing in the Bible and the Old Testament Apocrypha. She is in *Proverbs* 8 and 9, *Ecclesiasticus* 24, and elsewhere, decorously subordinated to Yahweh of course, but still female and strangely encroaching here and there on the preserves of the Holy Spirit.

Christianity began as a male religion. Like the Judaism from which it sprang, it vested a monopoly of miracle-working in God. Yet God's monopoly came to be modified, and it is interesting once again to recall how. Popular worship enthroned God's Mother Mary as a successor to all the goddesses. She became the one human being who was held to be perfectly attuned to the

Beyond; able, so to speak, to activate it at will and cause miracles to happen. She could manifest herself to the faithful; she could inspire; she was sometimes mystically identified with the Wisdom figure. We have been over all this ground, but let us now note what was not explicitly stressed before, that the one human being for whom all barriers vanished was a woman.

Psychologists of the school of Jung would invoke what they call the 'anima'. In the male minds which have so long governed society, there is said to be a submerged feminine element. Allegedly, each man's unconscious draws together his experiences of women, and his wishes and ideals about them, into a unity which is a vital part of his psychological make-up. The anima is a source of dreams, fantasies, imaginative creations, characters in myth and fiction. Jung and his disciples see it, moreover, as the root of the profoundest inspirations and insights, as the key to self-knowledge and integration. It is their psychological version of the Muse, and a great deal more. The Virgin herself is one of the supreme anima-images.

Whether or not we accept this theory, it is striking that it brings us round towards the same point by a different route. If we take the further step already suggested, and regard the unconscious as (in part) an aspect of a higher self in the Beyond, we are closer still to the implications of myth and religion. Somehow, in that region, it is the Female that opens the door. Or at any rate, the opening of the door is associated with female motifs. Judaism and Christianity tried to exclude this factor, but its pressure was too strong for them. In Lamaistic Buddhism it appears as the *shakti*, the female partner who accompanies even the highest beings.

So perhaps a more miraculous life implies humans in better sexual balance, with the feminine element enjoying its proper freedom. Conversely, if society progresses in that direction, we may hope to see the miraculous quietly expanding and flourishing.

198

Adams, Henry, *Mont-Saint-Michel and Chartres*. Constable, 1913.

Andrews, George, *Drugs and Magic*. Panther Books, 1975.

Ashe, Geoffrey, *The Ancient Wisdom*. Macmillan, 1977.
—— *The Land and the Book*. Collins, 1965.
—— *The Virgin*. Paladin, 1977.

Astrua, Massimo, *Illustrated Story of Lourdes*. Trans. Antonia Fumagalli. Catholic Publishing Co., 1975.

Cavendish, Richard, *The Black Arts*. Pan Books, 1969. See also *Man, Myth and Magic*.

David-Neel, Alexandra, *With Mystics and Magicians in Tibet*. John Lane, The Bodley Head, 1931.

Davis, Elizabeth Gould, *The First Sex*. Penguin Books, 1975.

Dodds, E. R., *The Greeks and the Irrational*. University of California Press, 1951.

Evans-Wentz, W. Y., *The Tibetan Book of the Great Liberation*. Oxford University Press, 1954.
—— *Tibetan Yoga and Secret Doctrine*. Oxford University Press, 1958.

Eysenck, H. J., 'Planets, Stars and Personality,' in *New Behaviour*, May 29th, 1975.

Ginzberg, Louis, *The Legends of the Jews*. 7 vols. Jewish Publication Society of America, Philadelphia, 1947.

Graef, Hilda, *Mary: a History of Doctrine and Devolution*. 2 vols. Sheed and Ward, 1963, 1965.

Herolt, Johannes, *Miracles of the Blessed Virgin Mary*. Trans. C. C. Swinton Bland. Routledge, 1928.

Kendrick, T. D., *Mary of Agreda*. Routledge & Kegan Paul, 1967.

Koestler, Arthur, *The Roots of Coincidence*. Pan Books, 1974.

Lawton, John Stewart, *Miracles and Revelation*. Lutterworth, 1959.

Lewis C. S., *Miracles*. Geoffrey Bles, 1947.

Liguori, St Alphonsus, *The Glories of Mary*. Trans. anon. Redemptorist Fathers, 1852.

Man, Myth and Magic (ed. Richard Cavendish). 7 vols. BPC Publishing Ltd., 1970–2.

Maraini, Fosco, *Secret Tibet*. Trans. Eric Mosbacher. Hutchinson, 1952.

Martindale, C. C., *The Message of Fatima*. Burns Oates & Washbourne, 1950.

Miegge, Giovanni, *The Virgin Mary*. Trans. Waldo Smith. Lutterworth, 1955.

Monden, Louis, *Le Miracle, Signe de Salut*. Desclée de Brouwer (Brussels), 1960.

Moule C. F. D. (ed.), *Miracles: Cambridge Studies in their Philosophy and History*. Mowbray, 1965.

Nostradamus. *The Prophecies of Nostradamus*. Ed. and trans. Erika Cheetham. Corgi Books, 1975.

Olivieri, A., and Billet, Bernard, *Y a-t-il encoure des Miracles à Lourdes?* P. Lethielleux (Paris), 1972.

Ouspensky, P. D., *In Search of the Miraculous*. Routledge & Kegan Paul, 1950.

Richardson, Alan, *The Miracle-Stories of the Gospels*. SCM Press, 1941.

Roerich, Nicholas, *Altai-Himalaya*. Jarrolds, 1930.

—— *Himalayas, Abode of Light*. David Marlowe, 1947.

Taylor, John, *Superminds*. Macmillan, 1975.

Tocquet, Robert, *The Magic of Numbers*. Trans. Denis Weaver, Elek, 1960.

Underhill, Evelyn, *The Miracles of Our Lady Saint Mary*. Heinemann, 1908.

Walsh, John, *The Shroud*. W. H. Allen, 1964.

West, D. J., *Eleven Lourdes Miracles*. Gerald Duckworth, 1957.

Wilson, Colin, *The Occult*. Hodder and Stoughton, 1971.

—— *Strange Powers*. Random House (New York), 1973.

Zola, Émile, *Lourdes*. Trans. Ernest Alfred Vizetelly. Chatto and Windus, 1929.

Index

202

203

Mary—contd.
    special relationship to God,
    80, 82–7, 92, 94–5, 97, 99,
    154–5, 194–5, 197–8; sup-
    posed attributes, 92–3, 98;
    apparitions of, 99, 101–5,
    114–16, 122–3; Fatima
    miracle, 114, 116–20;
    outside Christianity, 121–
    123; possible implications
    of cult, 123, 197–8
Maugham, W. Somerset, 70
Messiah, 48–9, 50, 51–2, 57–
    58, 144
Mind: lamaistic ideas of,
    136–7, 139, 142, 149, 154,
    193–4; in 'Inner Space',
    190–93
Mini-miracles, 164, 171, 172,
    173, 176–7, 186–7, 189–90,
    195, 196
Miracles: meaning of term,
    and supposed nature, 7–8,
    9, 11–13, 16–17, 26–9, 34,
    47, 107, 173, 176–7, 196;
    in Old Testament, 22–4,
    32–3, 36–42, 45–7; in
    Christianity generally, 51–
    57, 63–4, 70, 134–5, 149–
    150, 154–5, 173, 177, 194,
    195; spurious ones in
    Christian setting, 70–71;
    those attributed to Mary,
    79–80, 86–91, 93, 95–7,
    (at Lourdes) 104–12, 176,
    (at Fatima) 114, 116–20,
    140, 149, 151, 173: in Is-
    lam, 124–6; in other Asian
    systems, 126–7, 129, 131–
    135; views of lamas on,
    137, 138, 154–5, 156, 193–
    194; in relation to magic
    and the paranormal, 24–5,

164, 171, 173, 175–8, 189–90
Miriam, 39
Misraki, Paul, 122
Mohammed, 124–5
Mongolia, 136, 139, 142,
    144, 146
Moses, 21–4, 28, 32, 38–9,
    40, 46, 156
Munchausen, Baron, 70

Naples, 76
Nebuchadnezzar, 37–8
New Statesman, 123, 157
Nostradamus, 164

Occultism, 131, 156, 160,
    161, 197
Ogilvy, St John, 74
Old Testament, character of
    miracle-stories in, 36–42, 45
Oughtred, William, 162–3,
    191
Ouspensky, P. D., 27

Pandarus, 19
Paranormal, the, 14, 25–6,
    65, 156, 166–73, 189
Parapsychology, 25, 160
Paul, St, 75
Pauli, Wolfgang, 174
Peter, St, 64
Peyramale, Abbé, 103–4
Philistines, 37
Philostratus, 56
Pio, Padre, 68–9
Pius IX, 97
Pius XII, 97, 98
Polycarp, St, 74
Pontmain, 99
Prayer, answers to, 44–5,
    175, 177–8
Probability, 163–5, 174
Protestants, attitude to mir-
    acles, 65